Contents

Preface, ii

Microcomputer Programs, 1
  Susan M. Smith, El Paso, Texas

Divisibility, 5
  Clarence J. Dockweiler, Texas A. & M University, College Station, Texas

Magic Squares, 10
  E. Glenadine Gibb, University of Texas at Austin
  Vincent P. Schielack, Jr., University of Texas at Austin

Pentominoes, 16
  Charlotte L. Kessler, Griffith, Indiana

The History of Mathematics, 28
  Zalman Usiskin, University of Chicago, Chicago, Illinois

The Metric System, 31
  Janelle A. Elrod, Troy State University, Troy, Alabama

Mathematics and Home Economics, 35
  Jane F. Schielack, Texas A. & M. University, College Station, Texas
  Carolyn Klein, Texas Education Agency, Austin, Texas

Stamps That Depict History and Mathematicians, 39
  Martin H. Kessler, Griffith, Indiana

Tangrams, 42
  Edna F. Bazik, Normal, Illinois

Applications of Mathematics in Nursing, 51
  Lloyd I. Richardson, University of Missouri, Saint Louis, Missouri
  Judith Knight Richardson, Saint Louis Community College, Saint Louis, Missouri

Exploring Angles, 62
  Joel Schneider, Children's Television Workshop, New York, New York

Explorations in Modular Arithmetic, 74
  J. Paul McLaughlin, Purdue University Calumet, Hammond, Indiana

Investigating Programming Languages, 82
  Betty Travis, University of Texas at San Antonio

Archimedes, 86
  Robert Buss, Parkway West High School, Chesterfield, Missouri

Ancient Numeration Systems, 89
  George H. Willson, North Texas State University, Denton, Texas

Preface

Projects to Enrich School Mathematics (former title: *Student Merit Awards*) is a series of challenging research projects that provides enrichment material in a convenient format. In general, Level 1 is directed to upper elementary school students, Level 2 to middle school, and Level 3 to secondary school. The topics either are not found in the standard curriculum or represent a more in-depth study of standard topics. Most of the units contain material familiar to many teachers—material they would like to include in lessons but for which they never seem to have the time.

Teachers can either assign units to be done or allow students to select those that interest them. Care should be taken to match topics with the student's mathematical maturity. Units vary in length; most require between ten and thirty hours of outside research and writing. Many of the references can be found in school libraries and some in public or nearby college libraries. Students may occasionally need to consult people from the community or nearby colleges for information. Teachers should require students to credit their sources of information.

Each unit is composed of largely independent projects to be completed. A "guide" following many projects furnishes some essential information or hints and may also include drawings to present crucial information. The references are listed near the end of the unit. Many of the units include ideas for further investigations. These are meant to be motivational and may or may not be required by the teacher.

The material has been put into reproducible form for student use. The teacher notes for each unit include key information and solutions when appropriate. This section should be kept secure from the students.

This program was originally organized with the cooperation of five affiliated groups. Thanks go to the following representatives, who helped to acquire authors.

- Jennifer Smith, Missouri Council of Teachers of Mathematics
- Shirley Przybylski, Illinois Council of Teachers of Mathematics
- Gloria Donaldson, Alabama Council of Teachers of Mathematics
- J. Paul McLaughlin, Northern Indiana Council of Teachers of Mathematics
- Patsy Johnson, Texas Council of Teachers of Mathematics

Special thanks go to Jane Martin and Richard Lodholz for the long hours spent in reviewing and helping to edit the manuscript. Without their help and advice, this book would not have been finished.

Microcomputer Programs

SUSAN M. SMITH

COMPUTERS are an everyday part of business, government, and industry. Our lives are affected directly and indirectly by these machines that store large amounts of data, calculate accurately with astounding speed, provide instruction, play games, make decisions, and do many other tasks. With the availability of microcomputers at reasonable prices, it is generally believed that computers will become as much a part of our lives as the television or the telephone. This is already evident when we see such adaptations of microcomputers as computerized cash registers and video games.

The purpose of this unit is to acquaint you with what a computer program looks like and to get you started writing your own computer programs. Programming a computer allows you to communicate with the computer and make it do what you want it to do. *You* will then be telling the machine what to do rather than always following instructions written by someone else.

Projects

Project 1

1. List five uses of computers.
2. Identify the major components of a computer and describe briefly the function of each.
3. Explain what a computer program is.

Guide: Most introductory computer books will provide you with this information; the school library probably has books on computers. The public libraries generally have a larger number of books on computers. The references at the end of this unit might help.

Project 2

Type and run the following program on a computer. Choose three whole-number values for N and determine which numbers are to be printed.

```
10   INPUT N
20   FOR J = 2 TO N
30   F = N/J
40   IF F = INT(F) THEN 70
50   NEXT J
60   END
70   PRINT J
80   N = F
90   GO TO 20
```

Guide: The best way to do this is to use a computer that has floating point BASIC. Most computer stores will allow interested students to use their machines for short periods of time. The following explanation may give you some insight.

After the program is typed in, you need to type RUN. At this point a "?" appears on the screen. Line 10 causes the computer to wait for a value for N. Suppose you choose a number like 18 for N. The computer will execute the program in the following manner.

```
10   Type in 18; N then is equal to 18
20   The first J is 2
30   F = 18/2 = 9
40   Since F is an integer, go to line 70
70   2 appears on the screen
```

NCTM Projects to Enrich School Mathematics: Level 2

Line	Description
80	N now becomes 9
90	Go back to line 20
20	J is still 2
30	F = 9/2 = 4.5
40	F is not an integer, so go to the next line
50	J changes to 3, and this step leads back to line 20
20	Since J is not larger than N = 9, continue
30	F = 9/3 = 3
40	F is an integer, so line 70
70	3 appears on the screen
80	N = 3
90	To line 20
20	J = 3
30	F = 3/3 = 1
40	F is an integer
70	3 appears on the screen
80	N = 1
90	To line 20
20	Since N is 1, J cannot be between 2 and 1, and this leads to line 60
60	The program ends

Project 3

Type and run the following program on a computer. Choose several different whole-number values for A and B and go through the steps of this program to determine the output and purpose of the program.

```
10   INPUT A, B
20   L = 1
30   FOR J = 2 TO A
40   F = A / J
50   IF F = INT(F) THEN 100
60   NEXT J
70   L = A * B * L
80   PRINT L
90   END
100  G = B / J
110  IF G = INT(G) THEN 130
120  GO TO 60
130  L = J * L
140  A = F
150  B = G
160  GO TO 30
```

Guide: Use the same procedures as in Project 2. Notice in line 10 that two numbers, A and B, are entered. The "*" in line 70 means to multiply the numbers together.

Project 4

Write and test a program that will find the greatest common factor (GCF) of two whole numbers.

Guide: This program can be very similar to the one listed in Project 3. In fact, if you eliminate one particular line from that program, you will have the GCF.

Project 5

Write and test a program to reduce a fraction to its lowest terms.

Guide: You may wish to use A and B to represent the fraction A/B. The program in Project 4 will find the GCF of these two numbers. Then if both A and B are divided by the GCF, the fraction will be in lowest terms. *Hint:* This program can be done with only two revisions to your GCF program.

Project 6

Write and test a program to multiply two fractions together and then reduce the fraction to its lowest terms.

Guide: Consider two fractions, such as 2/3 and 3/8. To multiply them together, multiply the numerators together and then multiply the denominators. If the first fraction is represented by *N1/D1* and the second by *N2/D2*, then their product could be *A/B* where $A = N1 * N2$ and $B = D1 * D2$. Then the answer *A/B* can be reduced by using the program you wrote in Project 5.

Project 7

Write and test a program to add two fractions together and reduce the answer to lowest terms.

Guide: For all fractions of the form *a/b* and *c/d,* the sum will equal

$$\frac{ad + bc}{bd}$$

Notice that this form does not always use the smallest common denominator, but it will give a correct answer. For example, if the problem is 3/4 + 5/6, using this method we get

$$\frac{3*6 + 5*4}{4*6}, \text{ or } \frac{18 + 20}{24},$$

or 38/24. This fraction can then be reduced to its lowest terms using your previous program.

Further Investigations

PRINT statements could be added to each program to indicate exactly what should be entered in the computer and what is being printed on the screen. You may wish to try adding these statements to each program.

Many microcomputers have a graphics capability. By studying such a computer's programming manual, you can discover how to draw a line or create other geometric shapes on the screen. You can make the computer do many other things for you with additional study and practice.

REFERENCES

1. Albrecht, Robert L., Eric Lindberg, and Walter Mara. *Computer Methods in Mathematics.*
2. Albrecht, Robert L., Don Inman, and Ramon Zamora. *TRS-80 BASIC.* New York: John Wiley & Sons, 1982.
3. Bell, Marion J., and Sylvia Charp. *Be a Computer Literate.*
4. Dwyer, Thomas A., and Michael S. Kaufman. *A Guided Tour of Computer Programming in BASIC.* Boston: Houghton Mifflin Co., 1973.
5. Peckham, Herbert D. *BASIC: A Hands-On Method.* New York: McGraw-Hill Book Co., 1981.
6. Poirot, James L., and David Groves. *Computers and Mathematics.* Austin, Tex.: Sterling Swift, 1979.
7. Rice, Jean. *My Friend the Computer.* Minneapolis: T. S. Denison & Co., 1981.

Teacher Notes

All the programs listed here were tested on an APPLE II microcomputer with APPLESOFT. They should work on any machine with floating point BASIC. The programs do not necessarily represent the most efficient way of doing each task. Students should be encouraged to test, change, and add to any program.

Project 1

1. Five uses of computers
   - Class scheduling
   - Payrolls
   - Predicting weather
   - Controlling traffic lights
   - Inventory control
2. Major components of a computer
   - Input—device through which information is entered into a computer
   - Storage—device for saving or storing data within a computer system
   - Processor—device or system for performing operations on the data
   - Output—device for taking data from a computer and presenting them to the user
   - Control—unit for directing the flow of data to and from the various computer components in accordance with the instruction of the program
3. Explanation of a program: a detailed set of sequenced instructions telling the computer what to do

Project 2

This program finds the prime factors of any whole number N. Thus for $N = 18$ the numbers shown on the screen are 2, 3, and 3.

Project 3

This program finds the least common multiple for any two whole numbers A and B. For example, if $A = 12$ and $B = 15$, the value for L that appears on the screen is 60.

Project 4

Delete line 70.

Project 5

A complete program might be the following.

```
10   INPUT A, B
20   L = 1
30   FOR J = 2 TO A
40   F = A/J
50   IF F = INT(F) THEN 100
60   NEXT J
80   PRINT A, B
90   END
100  G = B/J
110  IF G = INT(G) THEN 130
120  GO TO 60
130  L = J * L
140  A = F
150  B = G
160  GO TO 30
```

Note: The only changes from the program in Project 3 are in lines 70 and 80.

Project 6

A complete program might be the following.

```
10   INPUT N1, D1
20   INPUT N2, D2
30   A = N1 * N2
40   B = D1 * D2
50   PRINT A, B
60   FOR J = 2 TO A
70   F = A/J
80   IF F = INT(F) THEN 120
90   NEXT J
100  PRINT A, B
110  END
120  G = B/J
130  IF G = INT(G) THEN 150
140  GO TO 90
150  A = F
160  B = G
170  GO TO 60
```

Project 7

Change line 30 in Project 6:

```
30   A = N1 * D2 + N2 * D1
```

Divisibility

CLARENCE J. DOCKWEILER

GUESSING about number characteristics is intriguing. How can you tell if a number is prime? Do you know what a perfect number is? The number 1991 is a palindrome—do you know why? As you study mathematics, divisibility rules will appear. How do you know if a number is divisible by 4 or 9 or 11? Can you tell by just glancing at the number? The purpose of this unit is to acquaint you with some divisibility rules and why they work.

Projects

Project 1

List ten multiples in table form for each of the numbers 2, 4, 5, and 8 according to the following requirements:

1) Three of the ten should be greater than 50 but less than 100.
2) Three of the ten should be greater than 200 but less than 300.
3) The last four should be greater than 1000.

n	50 < multiples < 100	200 < multiples < 300	1000 < multiples
2			
4			
5			
8			

Guide: Multiples of a number are those numbers that can be divided by the given number with the result being a whole number. For instance, 91 is a multiple of 7 because 91 ÷ 7 is the whole number 13. Multiples can also be expressed as products. That is, 91 is a multiple of 7 because 91 can be expressed as 7 × 13, a product including 7 as a factor.

Project 2

1) For each of the numbers 4, 5, and 8, write the divisibility rule. If you don't remember or haven't heard them before, check for them in most junior high school mathematics texts.
2) Check the multiples you used in Requirement 1 for each of the divisibility rules. Do all your multiples of 4 satisfy the rule for 4? For 5? For 8?

Guide: Divisibility rules are statements that describe an easy way to tell if a number can divide another number by a whole number. For example, we know that 824 is divisible by 2 because the digit in the ones place is a 4 and it is divisible by 2. References 4 and 5 will be helpful.

Project 3

For three different pairs of your numbers divisible by 3, prove that the sum is also divisible by 3 as follows:

1) Express each number as a product of 3 × _____.
2) Add the two numbers in that form. (3 × _____ + 3 × _____.)
3) Can the answer be expressed as 3 × _____?

What about the general case? Will any number divisible by 3, (3 × _____), added to another number divisible by 3, (3 × _____), result in another number divisible by 3? Write a mathematical sentence showing that.

Do parts 1, 2, and 3 for a number divisible by 4 also.

    4) Will the sum of two numbers divisible by the same number always result in another number that is also divisible?

Guide: Suppose we consider two numbers that are both divisible by 2—say, 42 and 104. We know they are divisible by 2 because the ones digits are, and because

$$42 = 2 \times 21$$

and

$$104 = 2 \times 52.$$

What do we get if we add the two numbers?

$$42 + 104 = 146$$

Is 146 divisible by 2? Yes, because

$$146 = 2 \times 73.$$

Will this always work? That is, if we add two numbers that are divisible by 2, does it seem reasonable that we should get another number that is divisible by 2? We use our product names to help explain:

$$42 = 2 \times 21$$
$$104 = 2 \times 52$$

so

$$42 + 104 = (2 \times 21) + (2 \times 52),$$

and

$$(2 \times 21) + (2 \times 52) = (2 \times 73),$$

or

$$(2 \times 21) + (2 \times 52) = 2 \times (21 + 52)$$

As you may know, the mathematical name for that last statement is the *distributive property*.

Every number that is divisible by 2 can be expressed as 2 × _____. Suppose we use two expressions like that as names for two numbers that are divisible by 2. We add them:

$$(2 \times \underline{}) + (2 \times \underline{})$$

What is the result? Will the answer always be divisible by 2?

$$(2 \times \underline{}) + (2 \times \underline{}) = 2 \times (\underline{} + \underline{})!$$

Have we proved it for every pair of numbers divisible by 2?

How about your numbers from Project 1 that are divisible by 3? Add pairs of them. Is the answer divisible by 3? Will the sum of two numbers that are divisible by 3 always be divisible by 3?

Project 4

    1) Write mathematical sentences that show that 200, 300, and 700 are all divisible by 4.
    2) Write a statement that shows that *every* multiple of 100 is divisible by 4.
    3) Write mathematical sentences that show that 6000, 7000, and 9000 are all divisible by 8.
    4) Write a statement that shows that *every* multiple of 1000 is divisible by 8.

Guide: Multiples of 10 (40, 70, etc.), multiples of 100 (200, 300, etc.), and multiples of 1000 (6000, 7000, etc.) are important multiples. When considering numbers divisible by 2 and 5, it is interesting to note that *every* multiple of 10 is also divisible by 2 (40 = 2 × 20) and divisible by 5 (40 = 5 × 8). That is true because 10 is divisible by both 2 and 5. References 4 and 5 will also be helpful here.

Project 5

1) The divisibility rule for 4 focuses on the number in the tens and ones place. That renames the number into a multiple of 100 plus the rest. For example, is 324 divisible by 4? Yes, because 24 is! That means that 324 = 300 + 24.

    Questions:
    Is 300 divisible by 4? _____ Why?
    Is 24 divisible by 4? _____ Why?
    Therefore, is the sum of 300 + 24 divisible by 4? _____ (Project 3)

2) Write similar mathematical sentences and questions for three of your numbers divisible by 4 from Project 1.

3) Why is it sufficient to look at the number in the tens and ones place to tell if the whole number is divisible by 4?

4) The divisibility rule for 8 focuses attention on the number formed by the last three digits of a number. For example, is 6528 divisible by 8? Yes, because 528 is! That renames the number into a multiple of 1000 plus the rest (6528 = 6000 + 528).

    Questions:
    Is 6000 divisible by 8? _____ Why?
    Is 528 divisible by 8? _____ Why?
    Therefore, is the sum of 6000 + 528 divisible by 8? _____ (Project 3)

5) Write similar mathematical sentences and questions for three of your numbers divisible by 8 from Project 1.

6) Why is it sufficient to look at the number in the last three digits to tell if the whole number is divisible by 8?

Guide: The divisibility rule for 2 focuses attention on the ones digit only. That, in effect, renames every number into a multiple of 10 plus the ones digit. For example, is 68 divisible by 2? Yes, because 8 is. That means that 68 becomes 60 + 8.

Questions:
Is 60 divisible by 2? Yes. (from Project 4)
Is 8 divisible by 2? Yes. (because 8 = 2 × 4)
Therefore, is 60 + 8 divisible by 2? (from Project 3, is the sum of two numbers divisible by 2 also divisible by 2?)

Project 6

1) Write the divisibility rule for 3 and for 9.
2) Pick a four-digit number that is divisible by 9 (or by 3) and write an expanded form of the number that shows that it is divisible as indicated.

Guide: Divisibility rules for 3 or 9 introduce "sum of digit" rules. Even though the rules seem considerably different from divisibility rules for 2, 4, and 8, the proof that they work uses a similar approach.

In Project 5, divisibility by 2 was justified for 68 by using the expanded notation form of 60 + 8. Since 60 and 8 are both divisible by 2, the whole number is also. Divisibility by 3 or 9 may be justified in a similar way. References 2, 3, 4, and 5 will be useful for this project.

Project 7

Try to determine a divisibility rule for 11 and for other numbers, if they are available.

1) State the rules.
2) Show that the rules work on several numbers.

Guide: References 1, 6, and 7 will provide the necessary background.

REFERENCES

1. Engle, Jessie Ann. "A Rediscovered Test for Divisibility by Eleven." *Mathematics Teacher* 69 (December 1976): 669.
2. Johnson, Phillip E. "Understanding the Check of Nines." *Arithmetic Teacher* 26 (November 1978): 54–55.
3. McCaffrey, Kenneth J. "'Digital Sum' Divisibility Tests." *Mathematics Teacher* 69 (December 1976: 670–74.
4. National Council of Teachers of Mathematics. *Enrichment Mathematics for the Grades*. Twenty-seventh Yearbook of the NCTM, chap. 16. Washington, D.C.: The Council, 1963.
5. National Council of Teachers of Mathematics. *Numbers and Their Factors*. Topics in Mathematics for Elementary School Teachers, bk. 5. Washington, D.C.: The Council, 1964.
6. Szetela, Walter. "A General Divisibility Test for Whole Numbers." *Mathematics Teacher* 73 (March 1980): 223–25.
7. Yazbak, Najib. "Some Unusual Tests of Divisibility." *Mathematics Teacher* 69 (December 1976): 667–68.

Teacher Notes

This unit on divisibility is designed to permit students to begin to see relationships between numbers and to develop an intuitive understanding of number theoretic proof. As such, the activities should lead them down the "garden path" to a "discovered" conclusion. Consequently, answers to questions may not be numerical but, rather, a student's discussion of a preliminary attempt to formulate generalizations. These Teacher Notes, therefore, attempt to suggest some expected student responses.

Project 1

This first exercise simply asks students to record multiples of the numbers in categories. These multiples will be used in later analyses and they should be checked for accuracy and correct classification.

Project 2

Ideally, the students should generate their own divisibility rules, but for the sake of using standard expressions they should check appropriate references and simply record a clear statement of each rule. Each of the rules should be applied to the multiples generated in Project 1 to make sure divisibility rules are correctly applied.

Project 3

This activity is designed to have students develop the very important theorem which states that given two numbers divisible by a third, the sum of the two numbers will also be divisible by the third number. Students should be encouraged to try various pairs of numbers which are both divisible by a third number to establish this basic idea more firmly.

Project 4

These activities are important building blocks for the following projects. Although Project 4 only asks questions for the numbers 4 and 8, the ideas are transferable to others.

Project 5

This development is the basic element for the students' confirmation of divisibility rules. The idea that any multiple of 100 is divisible by 4 permits the conclusion that if a multiple of 100 is added to a two-digit number that is a multiple of 4, the sum is a multiple of 4. This essentially confirms the divisibility rule. The student efforts for this project should be checked carefully to correct student misunderstandings.

Project 6

This activity requires considerable insight. Appropriate references will be needed for study. The key to students' understanding is their recognition that *every* power of 10 (each place value) is 1 more than a multiple of 3 or 9.

That is,

$$10 = 9 + 1$$
$$100 = 99 + 1$$
$$1000 = 999 + 1$$

Therefore, a number like 234 satisfies the divisibility rule for 9 because it can be renamed as

$$234 = (2 \times 100) + (3 \times 10) + 4$$
$$= [2 \times (99 + 1)] + [3 \times (9 + 1)] + 4$$
$$= (2 \times 99) + (2 \times 1) + (3 \times 9) + (3 \times 1) + 4$$
$$= \underline{(2 \times 99)} + 2 + \underline{(3 \times 9)} + 3 + 4$$

The underlined expressions are multiples of 9 and the remaining "leftovers" add up to a multiple of 9; therefore, the whole number is a multiple of 9 using previous developments. Similar results may be obtained for divisibility by 3.

Project 7

This last activity is open-ended to permit the student to extend the divisibility idea to other numbers and to plant the seed of a question regarding the justification of such rules. The justification of the divisibility rule for 11 is similar to previous developments, and capable students could be encouraged to attempt it.

Magic Squares

E. GLENADINE GIBB
VINCENT P. SCHIELACK, JR.

WHAT makes a magic square? *Magic square* is the name given to a figure in which the sum of the numbers in every row, every column, and in the two main diagonals is the same. The common sum is called the *magic number*. For the square in figure 1, the magic number is 15. The numbers used are 1, 2, 3, 4, 5, 6, 7, 8, and 9. This is an *ordinary magic square* because it consists of consecutive numbers starting with 1.

2	9	4
7	5	3
6	1	8

Fig. 1

Throughout history, people have been fascinated with magic squares. Some people do magic squares as a pastime; others, including mathematicians, have studied them for their special characteristics.

Projects

Project 1

Write a 250- to 500-word essay on the *history of magic squares*. Include information that provides answers to the following questions.

a) When and where were magic squares invented?

b) Why were people interested in them?

c) How did Benjamin Franklin become interested in magic squares? Did he make any specific discoveries about them?

d) What mathematicians have been interested in magic squares?

e) What is the formula for finding the magic number when the numbers are the first n consecutive numbers?

Guide: Using one or more sets of encyclopedias, look up the term *magic square*. You may also wish to look in other references. A reference list of looks for further reading and information follows Project 6. Undoubtedly you will locate other information about magic squares, including some methods for constructing them. You may wish to return to those resources when you are completing other projects. Remember that we shall not be doing *all* that can be done with magic squares in this unit and that you need not understand all that you read.

Project 2

Complete this project on *odd-ordered magic squares* by doing the following:

a) Construct a magic square using the numbers 2, 3, 4, 5, 6, 7, 8, 9, and 10. (*Hint:* Compare the magic number and the center number in the example given in fig. 1.) This magic square should be a *perfect magic square*, since the numbers are in sequence.

b) Construct an order-three magic square in which the numbers are not in sequence.

c) Construct an order-five magic square.

d) What instructions would you give to someone constructing an odd-ordered magic square? You may wish to try constructing more odd-ordered magic squares and refer to your resources before answering this question.

Guide: The *order* of a magic square is the number of rows (or columns) of cells of a magic square. Magic squares of order 3, 5, 7, 9, and so on, are *odd-ordered magic squares*. Magic squares of order 4, 6, 8, and so on are *even-ordered magic squares*. (See fig. 2.)

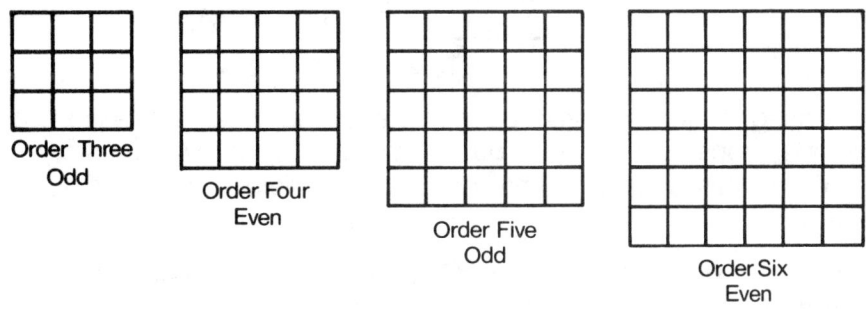

Fig. 2

Project 3

Finish the *incomplete* magic squares in figure 3. Find the numbers for the letters.

(a)
13	34	5	6	12
10	a	17	23	4
b	3	9	15	16
14	20	c	2	8
d	e	f	g	h

(b)
15	18	a	4	7
b	2	10	13	16
8	11	19	c	5
17	25	3	6	d
e	9	f	g	h

Fig. 3

Find the *error* in the square in figure 4.

(c)
47	56	34	22	83	7
24	67	44	26	13	75
29	52	3	99	18	48
17	49	89	4	53	37
97	6	33	11	74	28
35	19	46	87	9	54

Fig. 4

Project 4

For this project on *even-ordered magic squares,* you are to complete the following:

a) Construct an order-four magic square beginning with the number 1. What is the magic number?

b) Construct an order-four magic square in which the first number is not 1 but where the numbers follow the beginning number selected in sequence. What is the magic number of this 4 × 4 square?

c) Construct an order-four magic square using the numbers 0, 4, 8, and 12. The numbers must be repeated.

d) Construct an order-six magic square using the numbers 1–36. What is the magic number?

NCTM Projects to Enrich School Mathematics: Level 2

e) Construct an order-six magic square using the numbers 1, 2, 3, 4, 5, and 6. The square is started for you in figure 5. Of course, you must repeat numbers. What is the magic number?

1					6
	2			5	
		3	4		
		3	4		
	2			5	
1					6

Fig. 5

f) After constructing these even-ordered magic squares, what suggestions might you give someone interested in constructing one? You may wish to try more squares or consult your resources before answering this question. Write directions to help someone construct an even-ordered magic square.

Guide: The construction of even-ordered magic squares has always been more difficult than the construction of odd-ordered squares. Instead of having one center cell as in squares of odd order, the squares of even order have four center cells. As a starting point, however, putting numbers in consecutive order row by row from left to right produces a square that is magic in the diagonals. This procedure can be used for squares of even order but not for odd order. Then, it will usually be necessary to relocate the numbers that are not in the diagonals by trial-and-error methods. Perhaps you will discover a systematic way to place the other numbers in even-ordered magic squares.

Project 5

For this project on *equivalent magic squares,* construct both an order-three and an order-four magic square. They can be different from those you constructed in Projects 2 and 4. Call the order-three magic square "anchor 3" and the order-four magic square "anchor 4."

a) Turn each anchor magic square 90° clockwise about the center. Show your new order-three magic square. What is its magic number? Show your new order-four magic square. What is its magic number?

b) Construct a new square by adding 3 to each number in each cell of anchor 3. Examine your new square. Is it a magic square? How does its magic number compare with the anchor 3 magic number? Repeat by using anchor 4 magic square. Compare your new order-four magic square with anchor 4.

c) Construct a new order-three magic square and a new order-four magic square by adding −2 to each number in each cell of your anchor 3 and anchor 4 magic squares. Are your new squares magic squares? What is the magic number of each?

d) Construct a new order-three magic square and a new order-four magic square by multiplying each number in your anchor magic squares by 4. Are your new squares magic squares? What is the magic number of each?

If two magic squares are *equivalent,* they have a structure and internal relationship similar to the four order-three magic squares and the four order-four magic squares you have made. These were made by rotating, by adding, and by multiplying. If the magic squares are not equivalent, they are called *distinct magic squares.*

Project 6

For this project on *composite squares,* you need to complete the following:

1. Construct a 9 × 9 composite (order 9) magic square by completing the square started in figure 6.

    a) Use your formula from Project 1e to find the magic number of an ordinary magic square of order n, where $n = 9$.

b) Complete the composite square by entering the other eight 3 × 3 magic squares, using the numbers 1–81.

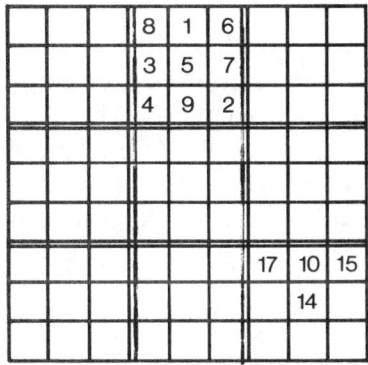

Fig. 6

2. Construct a composite 12 × 12 magic square using the magic square in figure 7 as your first entry. What is the magic number?

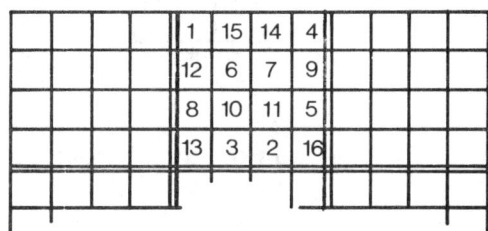

Fig. 7

Guide: One of the most useful ways of constructing a magic square is to produce the composite magic square—a magic square whose elements are magic squares. The smallest composite magic square is a 9 × 9 (order 9) magic square and consists of 3 × 3 (order 3) magic squares arranged in the same order as the numbers in the first subsquare. The first subsquare has been placed for you in figure 6. Note that the second subsquare goes in the lower right-hand corner and has been started. Observe the pattern between the numbers in the first subsquare and the second subsquare. The last subsquare occupies the middle section of the third horizontal row.

REFERENCES

1. Andrews, W. S. *Magic Squares and Cubes.* New York: Dover Publications, 1970.
2. Ball, W. W. R. *Mathematical Recreations and Essays.* Revised by H. S. M. Coxeter. New York: Macmillan Co., 1962.
3. Bowers, Henry, and Joan E. Bowers. *Arithmetical Excursions—an Enrichment of Elementary Mathematics.* New York: Dover Publications, 1961.
4. Cajori, Florian. *History of Mathematics.* 3d ed. New York: Chelsea Publishing Co., 1980.
5. Encyclopedia Americana. "Magic Squares."
6. Encyclopaedia Britannica. "Magic Squares."
7. Gardner, Martin, ed. *Second Scientific American Book of Puzzles and Diversions.* New York: Simon & Schuster, 1961.
8. Kraitchik, Maurice. *Mathematical Recreations.* New York: Dover Publications, 1953.
9. Smith, David Eugene. *History of Mathematics,* vol. 2. Boston: Ginn & Co., 1925.
10. Sobel, Max A., and Evan M. Maletsky. *Teaching Mathematics: A Sourcebook of Aids, Activities, and Strategies.* Englewood Cliffs, N.J.: Prentice-Hall, 1975.

Teacher Notes

Project 1

To complete parts a–d, the student is expected to have become familiar with the history of magic squares. Information can be found in encyclopedias, although students may wish to seek out other resources available in mathematics books in libraries. This project is expected to provide the student with the opportunity to seek out resources not only for use in fulfilling this project but also for those that follow. A list of references for further reading is provided at the end of the unit. Questions are provided, but students should not be limited to these questions. Constructing magic squares is not a part of this project.

e) $\dfrac{n^3 + n}{2}$, where n is the number of cells in a row.

Project 2

(a)
5	10	3
4	6	8
9	2	7

Magic number is 18.

(b)
16	2	12
6	10	14
8	18	4

Responses will vary.

(c)
8	1	24	17	15
5	23	16	14	7
22	20	13	6	4
19	12	10	3	21
11	9	2	25	18

Responses will vary.

Magic number is 65 for ordinary magic square.

d) Responses will vary.

Project 3

a) (a) 16
    (b) 27
    (c) 26
    (d) 6
    (e) −3
    (f) 13
    (g) 24
    (h) 30

b) (a) 21
    (b) 24
    (c) 22
    (d) 14
    (e) 1
    (f) 12
    (g) 20
    (h) 23

c) The error is in the last row; the number should be 8 instead of 9.

Project 4

Answers may vary.

(a)
1	15	14	4
12	6	7	9
8	10	11	5
13	3	2	16

Magic number is 34.

This answer is *one* possibility.

(b)
5	19	18	8
16	10	11	13
12	14	15	9
17	7	6	20

Magic number is 50.

(c)
0	8	4	12
12	4	8	0
12	4	8	0
0	8	4	12

Magic number is 24.

(d)
1	32	4	33	35	6
12	8	28	27	11	25
19	23	15	16	14	24
18	17	21	22	20	13
30	26	9	10	29	7
31	5	34	3	2	36

Magic number is 111.

(e)
1	5	4	3	2	6
6	2	4	3	5	1
6	5	3	4	2	1
1	5	3	4	2	6
6	2	3	4	5	1
1	2	4	3	5	6

Magic number is 21.

f) Students' directions will vary.

Project 5

Responses will vary depending on the anchor squares constructed.

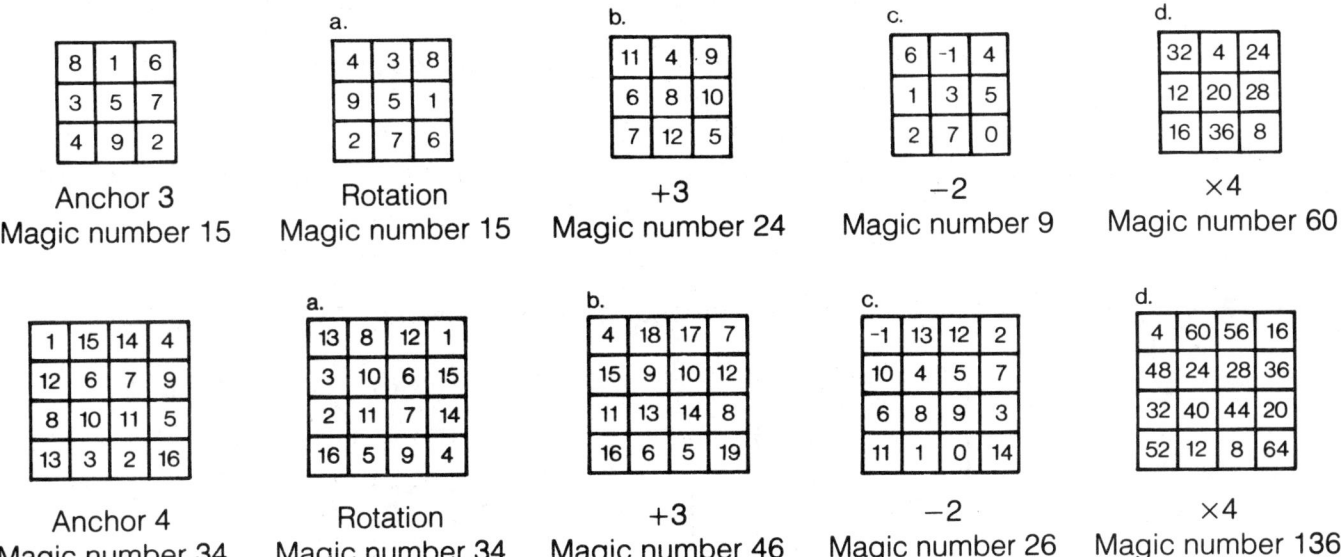

Project 6

1a. The magic number is 369.

(b)
71	64	69	8	1	6	53	46	51
66	68	70	3	5	7	48	50	52
67	72	65	4	9	2	49	54	47
26	19	24	44	37	42	62	55	60
21	23	25	39	41	43	57	59	61
22	27	20	40	45	38	58	63	56
35	28	33	80	73	78	17	10	15
30	32	34	75	77	79	12	14	16
31	36	29	76	81	74	13	18	11

Order-9 composite magic square

(2)
113	127	126	116	1	15	14	4	81	95	94	84
124	118	119	121	12	6	7	9	92	86	87	89
120	122	123	117	8	10	11	5	88	90	91	85
125	115	114	28	13	3	2	16	93	83	82	96
33	47	46	36	65	79	78	68	97	111	110	100
44	38	39	41	76	70	71	73	108	102	103	105
40	42	43	37	72	74	75	69	104	106	107	101
45	35	34	48	77	67	66	80	109	99	98	112
49	63	62	52	129	143	142	132	17	31	30	20
60	54	55	57	140	134	135	137	28	22	23	25
56	58	59	53	136	138	139	133	24	26	27	21
61	51	50	64	141	131	130	144	29	19	18	32

Order-12 composite magic square
Magic number is 870

NCTM Projects to Enrich School Mathematics: Level 2

Pentominoes

CHARLOTTE L. KESSLER

PUZZLES and geometric shapes have intrigued mathematicians for centuries. In 1953 S. W. Golomb entertained the Harvard Mathematics Club with a new puzzle that he called Pentominoes. During the next few years, pentominoes became very popular within the mathematics circle, sparking an addiction comparable to the modern Rubik's Cube. Hi-Q manufactured a commercial plastic version of the puzzle called Hexed. However, its nationwide popularity has been modest.

A word of caution if you decide to pursue this unit: pentominoes are definitely habit forming. Persons have been known to sacrifice sleep and food while searching for puzzle solutions.

A pentomino is a pattern of five connecting squares that share at least one common side.

An acceptable link:

Unacceptable links:

Using only four squares, you would arrive at these possible arrangements:

Projects

Project 1

Construct a pentomino set of the twelve possible arrangements of five squares.

Guide: Remember that the squares must be joined side to side. Draw your pentominoes on grid paper. Cut out the pieces and check for duplicates by rotating and flipping. Any shape that can be flipped or turned to fit on top of another is the same shape. You should have twelve *different* patterns of five squares.

Make the set by gluing the joined edges of sixty 2.2 cm × 2.2 cm squares. These are convenient dimensions, since the completed puzzle patterns will then fit nicely on 8½-by-11-inch paper. (Using 1″ × 1″ squares is a disadvantage, since many of the patterns will overflow regular notebook paper.) If possible make a set out of wood. A set may also be cut from cardboard, or a plastic commercial set may be purchased.

Project 2

Find the dimensions of the four possible rectangles that can be made using your set of pentominoes. Each rectangle must use all twelve pentominoes. Now complete the interior patterns for two of these rectangles.

Guide: The dimensions of a rectangle are its length and width. The area of a rectangle equals its length times its width. Each pentomino contains five square units, so you are searching for the possible whole numbers that will multiply to sixty square units of area (5 units × 12 pentomino patterns).

Ask yourself the following questions: Can you make a 2 × 30 rectangle? Can you make a 1 × 60 rectangle? Why? There are four possible dimensions for rectangles. What are they? (Reference 1 may help you.)

Project 3

Complete the given triplications, then make and complete three other triplications of your own.

Guide: Each pentomino can be enlarged by the ratio 1:3. The area of the unit square will be increased to nine square units. Each triplication outline will form a new puzzle to be solved by using nine of the twelve pentomino pieces. Can you complete the following four triplications?

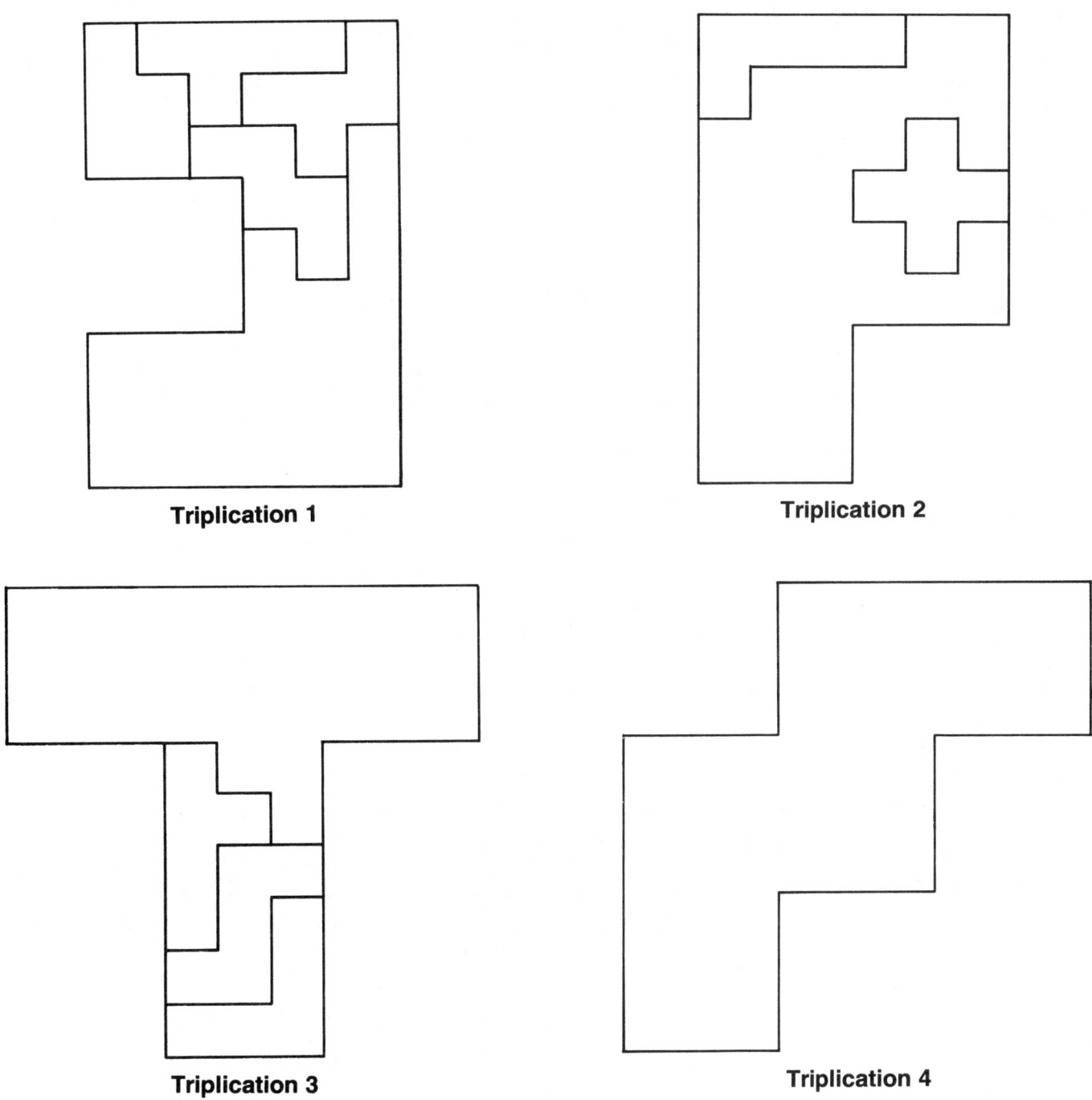

Triplication 1

Triplication 2

Triplication 3

Triplication 4

NCTM Projects to Enrich School Mathematics: Level 2

Use a straightedge and make the outline of the triplications for three other pentominoes. Remember that each side length is tripled. In other words, a length of 2.2 cm would become 6.6 cm. For example, if you want to triplicate

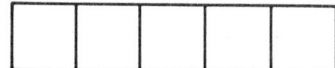

the enlarged dimensions would be 33 cm × 6.6 cm. You may want to use a protractor for the 90° angles.

Project 4

Form congruent shapes of four pentominoes each. Congruent polygons have the same size and shape. The twelve pentomino shapes can be divided into three sets (four pentominoes each), and each set of four can be used to form one of the three congruent polygons.

Guide: There are three different congruency puzzles to solve. The pentomino set has been divided for you in the first congruent-shape puzzle sheet. Work the puzzles and trace the solutions. In the third puzzle, the shaded square represents an interior hole and should not be covered.

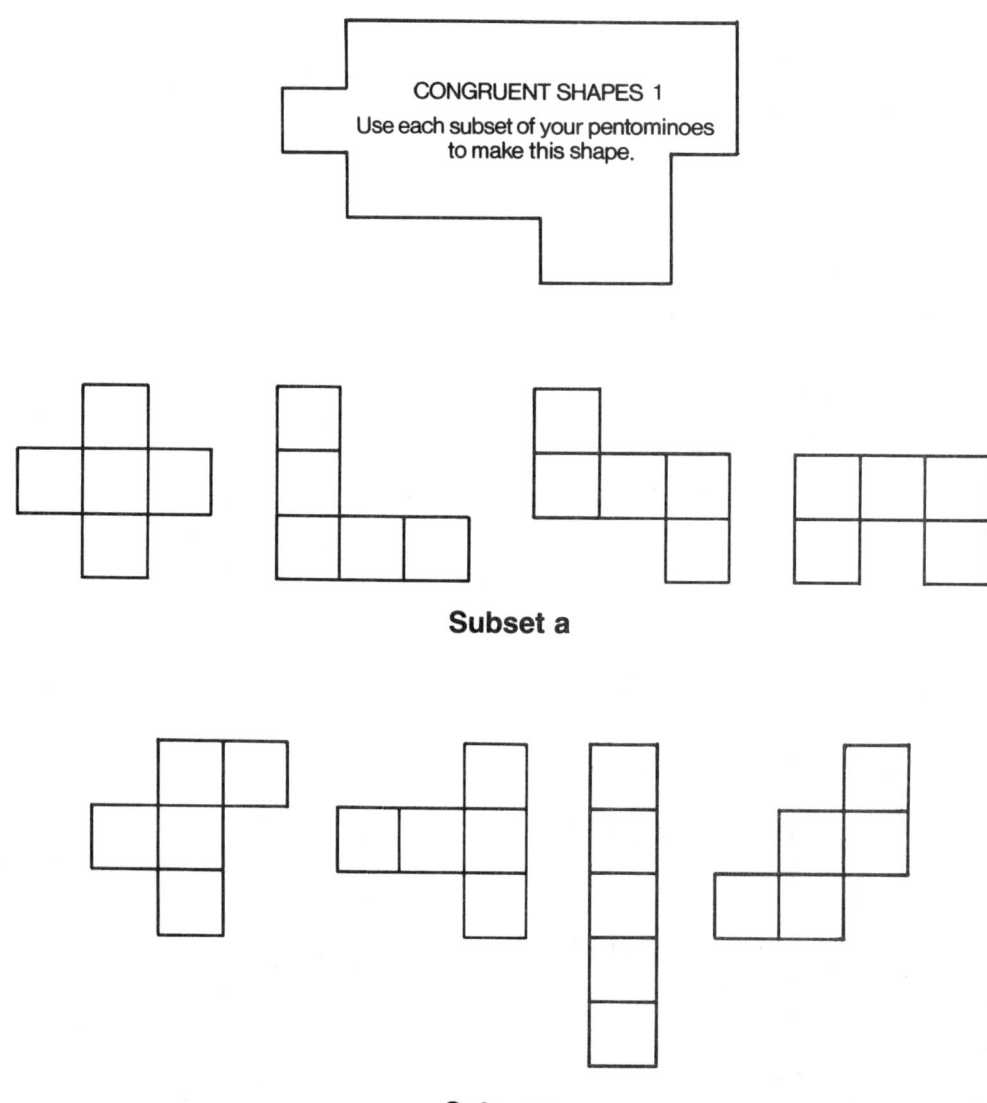

Subset a

Subset b

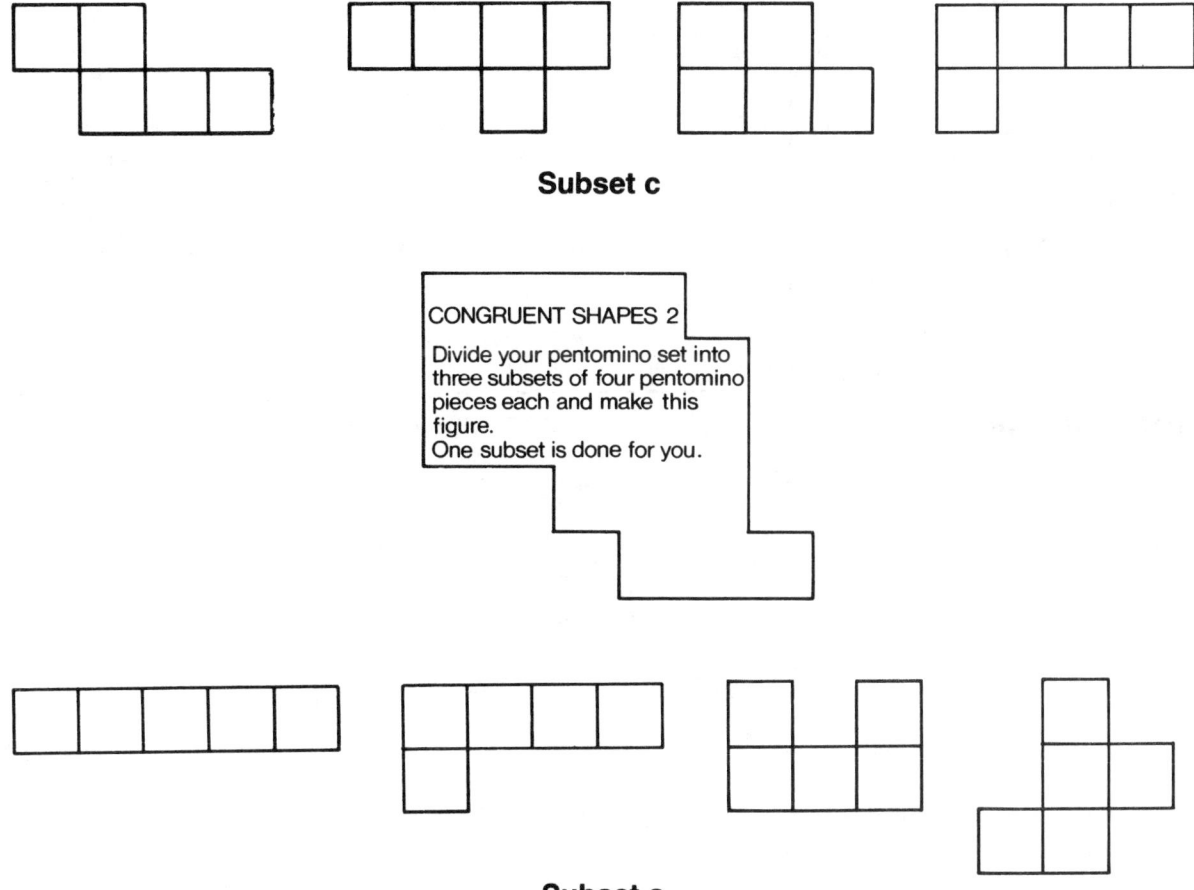

Subset c

Subset a

Now find subset b and c.

CONGRUENT SHAPES 3

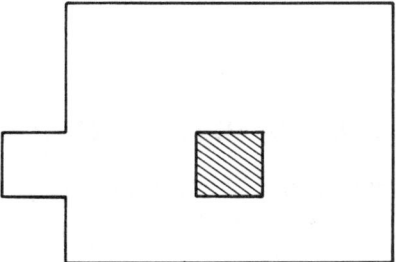

Find subsets a, b, and c.

Project 5

a) Solve one of the three challenge puzzles. Sketch the interior pattern of your solution.

b) Create a challenging puzzle of your own and show the solution.

Guide: The complete set of pentominoes can be used to make interesting polygons. Work one of the three puzzle challenges and then create a puzzle of your own to share with your classmates. (References 2 and 3 will help you.)

Puzzle Challenge 1 **Puzzle Challenge 2**

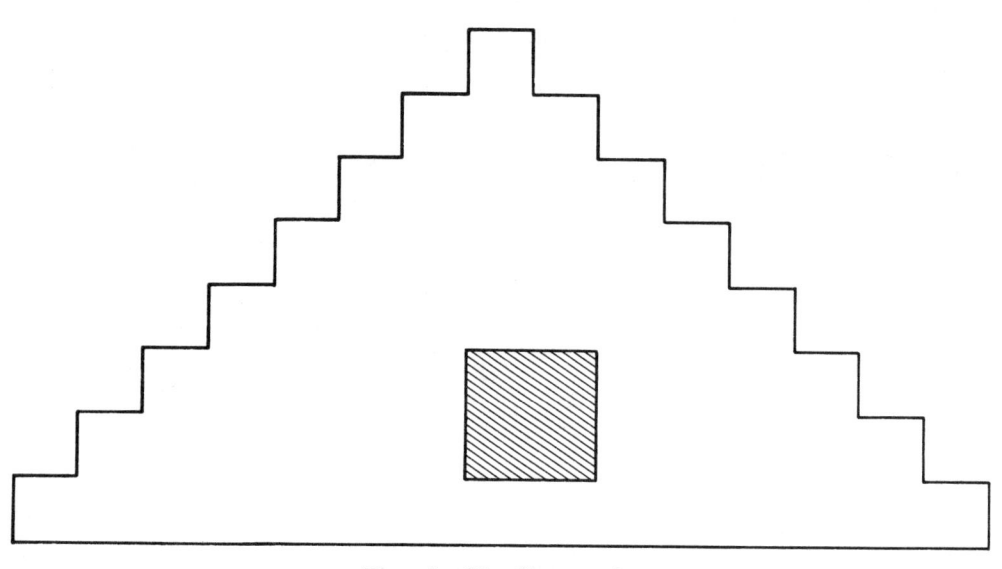

Puzzle Challenge 3

Further Investigations

Make a definition for a hexomino. How many hexominoes do you think there are? Use grid paper and sketch the possible hexominoes. (See Reference 2.)

REFERENCES

1. Fleenor, Charles R., Robert E. Eicholz, and Phares O'Daffer. *Investigating School Mathematics,* p. G-72. Reading, Mass.: Addison-Wesley, 1973–74.
2. Gardner, Martin. *Mathematical Puzzles and Diversions.* New York: Simon & Schuster, 1959.
3. Golomb, Solomon W. *Polyominoes.* New York: Charles Scribner's Sons, 1965.
4. Claasen, Ronald, and Arthur J. Wiebe. *Pentominoes.* Fresno, Calif.: Creative Teaching Associates, 1973.

Teacher Notes

The game Hexed has been distributed by Hi-Q, Kohner, and Gabriel. It can usually be purchased at a local toy or variety store. I have found several at flea markets and garage sales for very reasonable prices.

As the students work through the unit, encourage them to enlarge the miniature drawings to the scale of their puzzle. Once a student has a full-scale outline, the solution to the puzzle becomes easier. You might also suggest putting a frustrating puzzle away for a short time, since the solution may be easier at a later date.

For an in-depth look at polyomino theory, check *Recreational Mathematics Magazine,* issues 4–6, 8, and 10.

Project 1: The twelve pentominoes

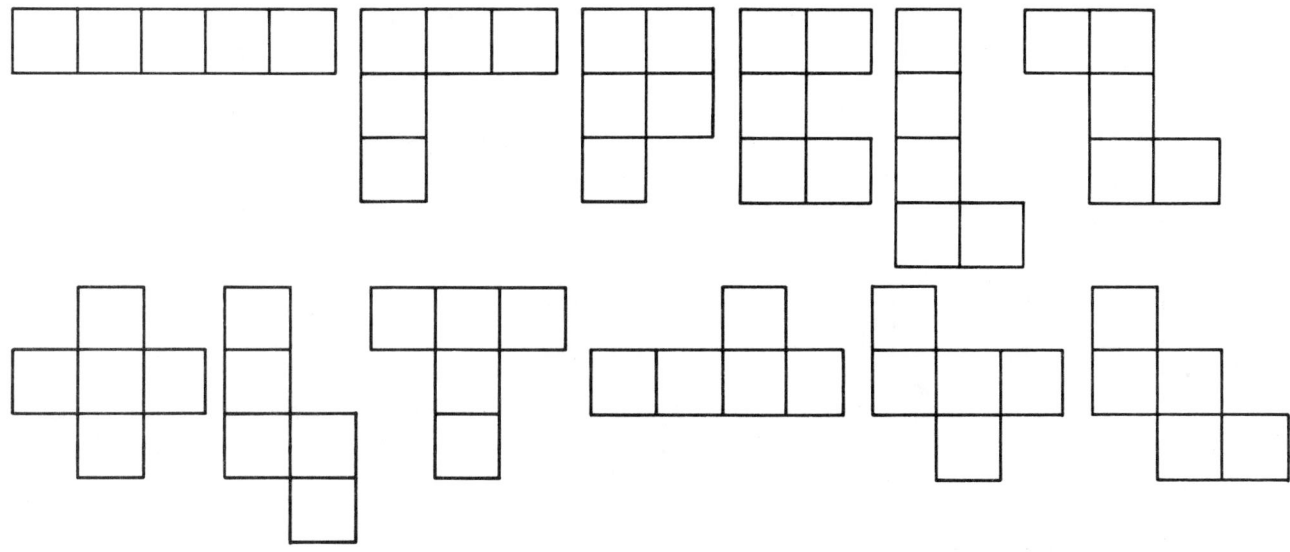

NCTM Projects to Enrich School Mathematics: Level 2

Project 2: Rectangle dimensions

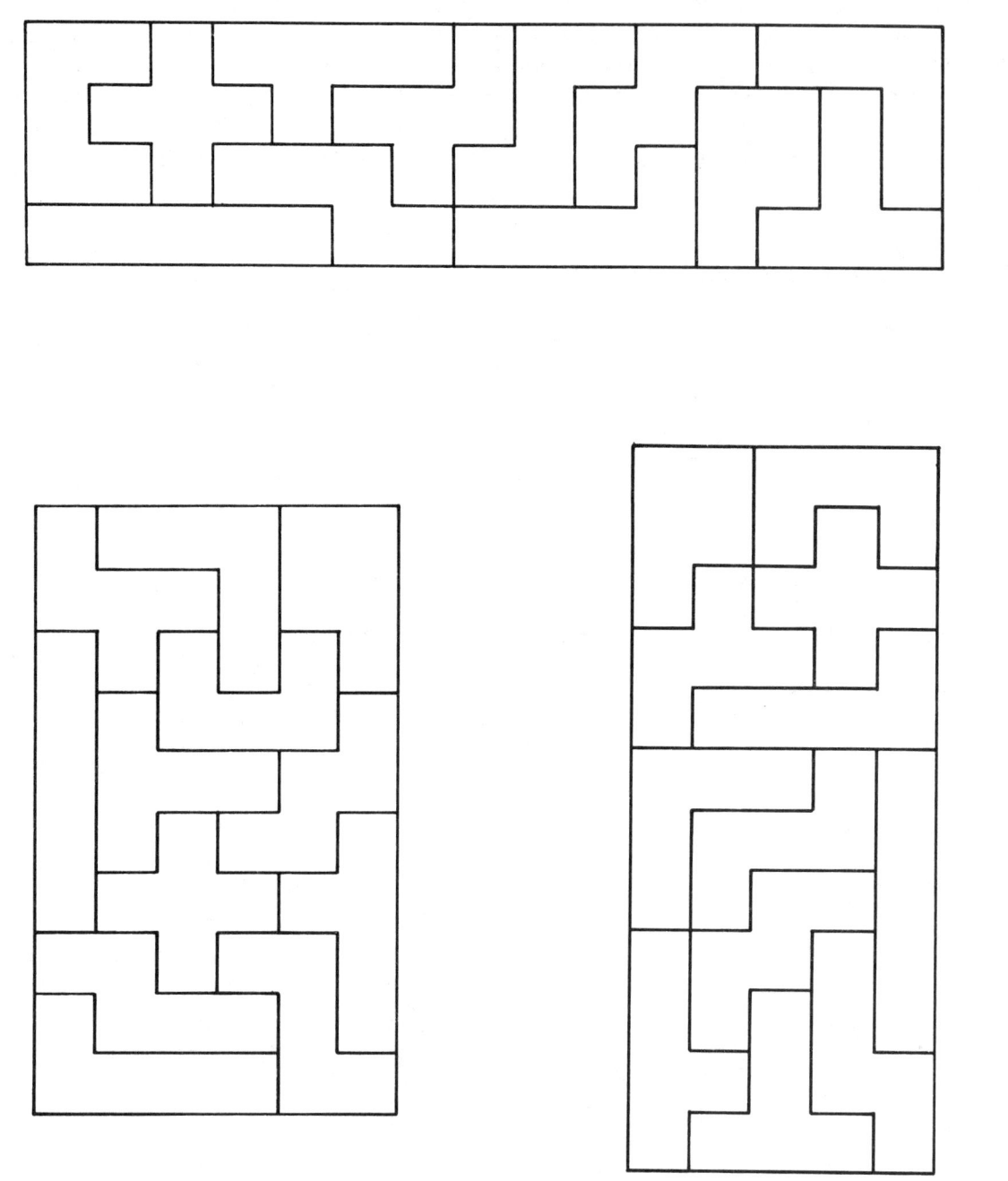

22   *NCTM Projects to Enrich School Mathematics: Level 2*

Project 3: Triplications

NCTM *Projects to Enrich School Mathematics: Level 2*

Project 3: Triplications—Continued

Project 4: Congruent shapes

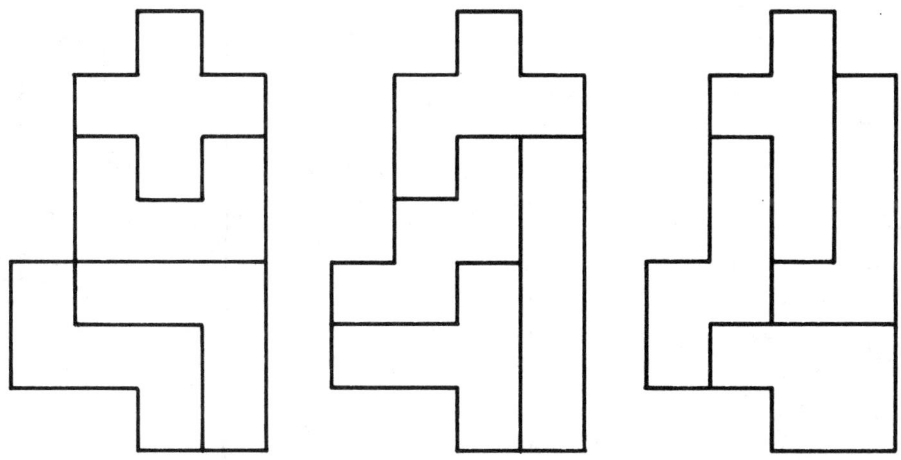

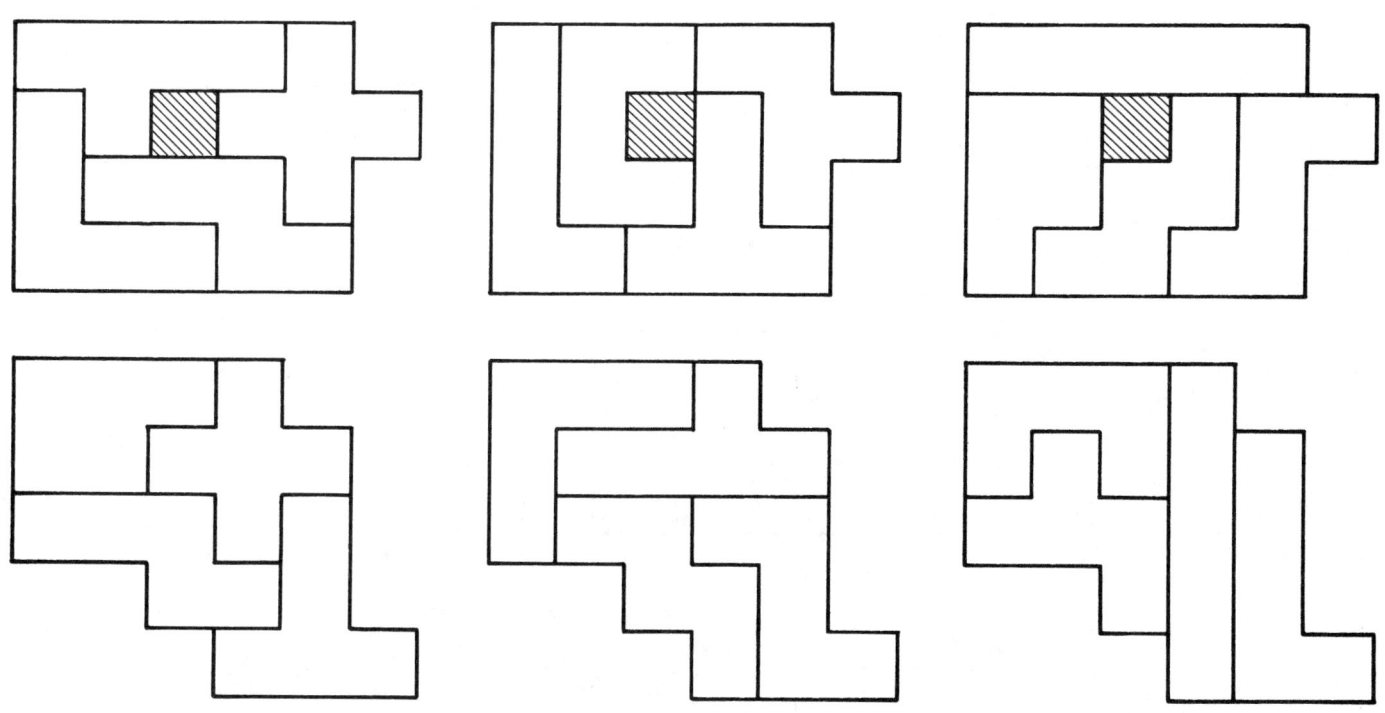

NCTM Projects to Enrich School Mathematics: Level 2

Project 5: Puzzle challenges

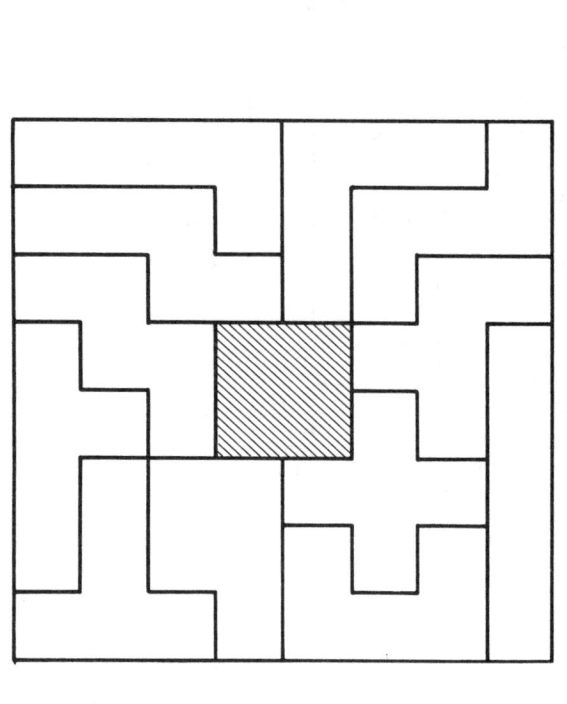
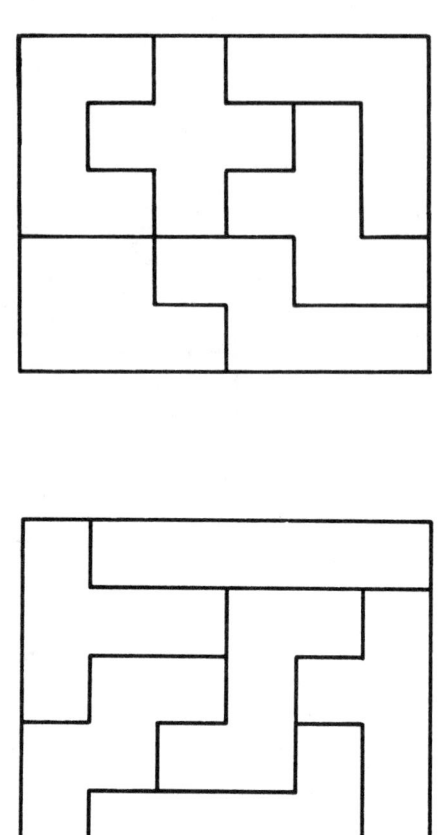
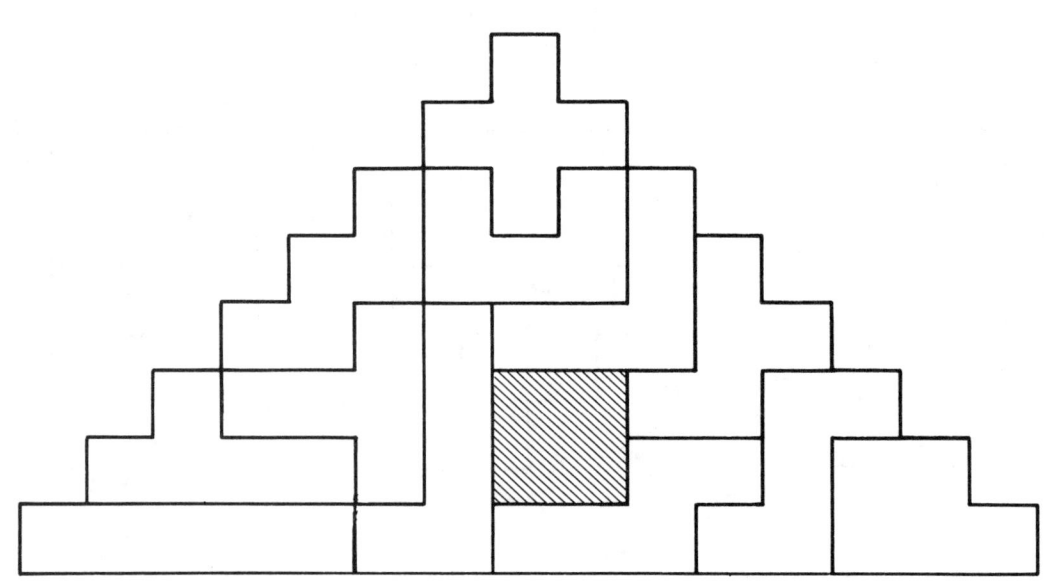

26   NCTM Projects to Enrich School Mathematics: Level 2

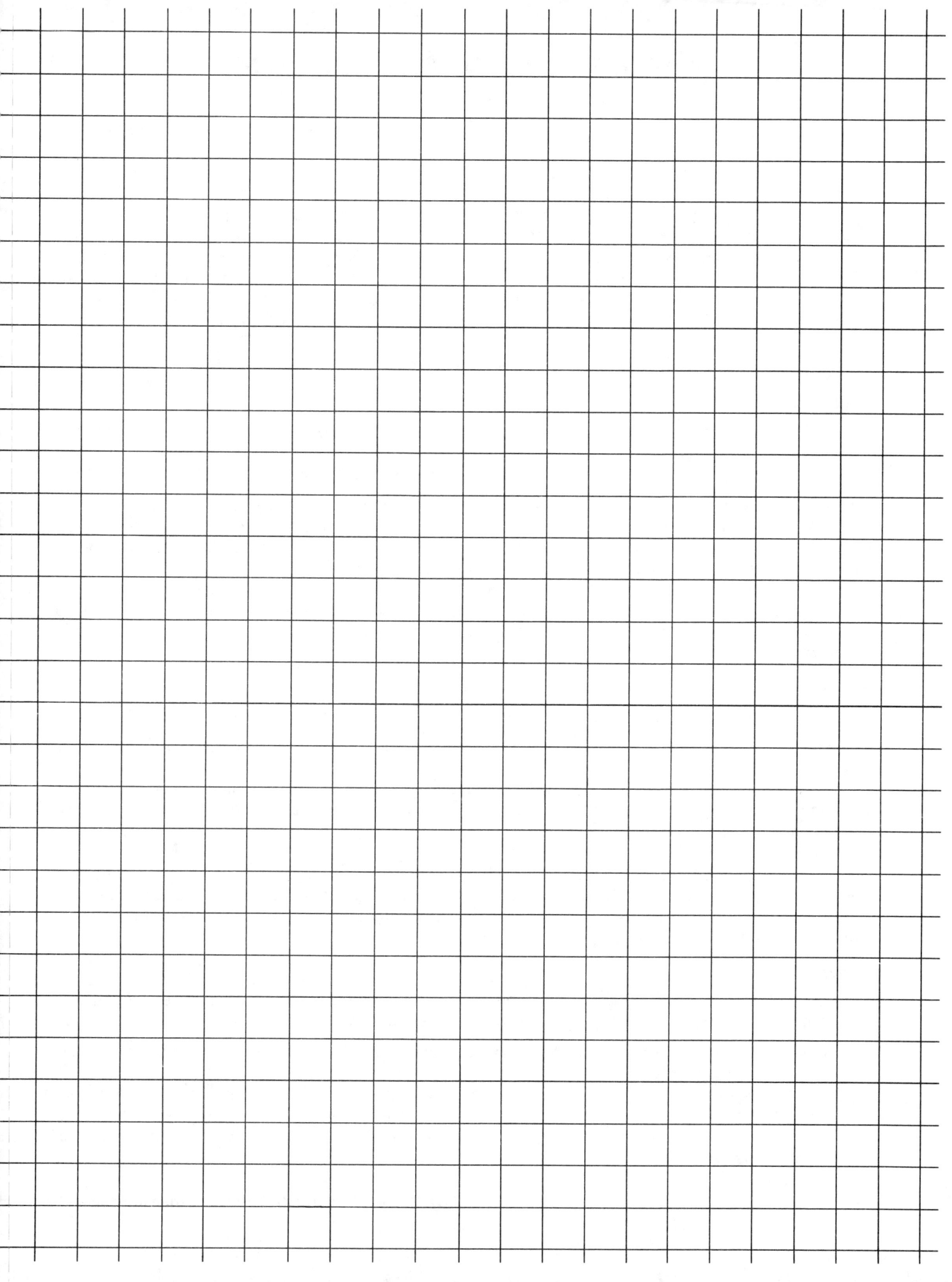

The History of Mathematics

ZALMAN USISKIN

AS EVERYONE knows, mathematics has a long history. We have records of people doing mathematical calculations as long as five thousand years ago. But what most people do not realize is that today's mathematics is quite new. The arithmetic you know was not known to most educated people until the 1700s, and many of the symbols you use, such as + and ×, were invented only a short time before that. The purpose of your work in this area is to acquaint you with some of the more important people in the development of mathematics and some specific events in the history of arithmetic.

Projects

Project 1

Identify ten of the following mathematicians by country and century of work, as well as naming one thing for which each is famous: Euclid, Gauss, Archimedes, Newton, Euler, Descartes, Leonardo of Pisa, Gödel, Russell, Cayley, Pythagoras, Brahmagupta, Thales, Viète, Riemann, von Neumann, Weyl.

Guide: References 2 and 4 will help you with this task, or you can find most of these mathematicians' work described in a large encyclopedia. Learn the first names of those who have them: this can help you remember their nationality. For example, Cayley's first name was Arthur, which is a hint that he was British, whereas Viète's first name was François, which suggests that he was French.

You do not have to understand the work for which the person is known. Just naming some mathematical things each person did is enough to satisfy this requirement. For example, you could say that von Neumann helped establish the branch of mathematics called game theory. You do not have to know what game theory is.

Project 2

Write an explanation of the numeration system used by (*a*) the Babylonians and (*b*) the Mayans.

Guide: Reference 4 will help you. Many books on the teaching of arithmetic also discuss these systems.

To complete this project you should be able to write the symbols that these cultures used to represent both small numbers (just like we use the symbols 1, 2, 3, etc.) and large numbers (we put together our symbols to write 12, 3321, etc.).

The Babylonians and Mayans lived in different parts of the world and in different times. Knowing the way one of these cultures represented numbers will not give you a hint about how the other one represented numbers. Although the Mayans lived closer to what is now the United States, the Babylonian system has had more influence on us today. The way we tell time and measure angles is based on the ways the Babylonians did these things.

Project 3

Our numerals 0, 1, 2, . . . , 9, 10, 11, 12, . . . are called Hindu-Arabic numerals. Write a description of the roles the Hindus and the Arabs played in the development of this system.

Guide: Use the same references as for Project 2. You can also find this information in books on world history or in encyclopedias.

This is an easy project to complete once you have the information. You should know which of these peoples developed the numerals and which helped spread the numerals to the Western world. You should also know what it was that caused these people to spread their culture, and you should know approximately when this happened.

You may be surprised to learn when our numerals were developed. Most people think they are a lot older than they really are.

Project 4

Give the approximate time of the invention of six of the following symbols: $=, +, \times, -, \div, \sqrt{}, \pi$.

Guide: You will find References 1, 2, or 3 helpful.

When you read about these symbols, it may help you to know that the first arithmetic book written in English was by Robert Recorde in 1557. It contained the first use of one of the symbols named above. You may not see the complete square root sign ($\sqrt{}$) as we in the United States use it. Europeans leave off the top bar and write $\sqrt{}2$, the way it was first used.

Project 5

Read biographies of the lives of two famous mathematicians and tell a group of people about them.

Reference 2, although filled with biographies of mathematicians, lists no women mathematicians. Reference 5 has biographies of some famous female mathematicians.

As you are telling people about the life of a mathematician, think about more than just the mathematics the person did. Report where the person was born, whether rich or poor, famous or unknown to contemporaries, educated formally or outside of school, a relative or friend of other mathematicians, and so on. Tell interesting stories about the person.

In the minds of some people, Evariste Galois and Srinivasa Ramanujan have the most interesting life stories of any mathematicians. References 6 and 7 can tell you more about them.

Project 6

Write a five-hundred-word essay describing some of the mathematics that has been developed in the twentieth century.

Guide: Reference 4 can get you started. Reference 6 will also help. Some of the mathematics discovered in this century requires advanced mathematics even to understand, so you should concentrate on those areas you can understand. An essay of five hundred words is about two pages long when it is typewritten and double-spaced.

Two developments you should be sure to mention are computers (including calculators and microcomputers) and statistics. Try to identify what it was that was developed, who developed it (if an individual was responsible), and when it happened.

Further Investigations

If you are interested in this topic, you might wish to go to the library and check out books dealing with the history of science. (In these books, mathematics is usually considered a part of science.)

History continues to be created. Today, many mathematicians work for colleges or universities. If you call the mathematics department of a college or university, you probably could talk to a person who could tell you what mathematicians do today. You could compare that with what you have read about the lives of famous mathematicians of the past.

REFERENCES

1. National Council of Teachers of Mathematics. *Historical Topics for the Mathematics Classroom.* Thirty-first Yearbook of the NCTM. Washington, D.C.: The Council, 1969.
2. Bell, Eric T. *Men of Mathematics.* New York: Simon & Schuster, 1937.
3. Cajori, Florian. *A History of Mathematical Notation.* 2 vols. 2d ed. La Salle, Ill.: Open Court Publishing Co., 1951, 1952.
4. Eves, Howard. *An Introduction to the History of Mathematics.* 4th ed. New York: Holt, Rinehart & Winston, 1976.
5. Perl, Teri. *Math Equals: Biographies of Women Mathematicians and Related Activities.* Reading, Mass.: Addison-Wesley Publishing Co., 1978.
6. Kline, Morris. *Mathematical Thought from Ancient to Modern Times.* New York: Oxford University Press, 1972.
7. Steen, Lynn A., ed. *Mathematics Today.* New York: Random House, 1980.

Teacher Notes

Project 1

Euclid	Greek	3d century B.C.
Karl Friedrich Gauss	German	1777–1855
Archimedes	Greek	287?–212 B.C.
Isaac Newton	English	1642–1727
Leonhard Euler	Swiss	1707–1783
René Descartes	French	1596–1650
Leonardo of Pisa (Fibonacci)	Italian	1180?–?1250
Kurt Gödel	Czechoslovakian/American	1906–
Bertrand Russell	British	1872–1970
Arthur Cayle	British	1821–1895
Pythagoras	Greek	5th century B.C.
Brahmagupta	Hindu	588–?660
Thales	Greek	640?–546 B.C.
François Viète	French	1540–1603
Georg Friedrich Bernhard Riemann	German	1826–1866
John von Neumann	Hungarian/American	1903–1957
Hermann Weyl	German	1855–1955

All these mathematicians are famous for more than one piece of work, but for most of them we list only one here. Euclid organized the known geometry of his time into a famous logical system. Gauss proved the fundamental theorem of algebra, namely, that every polynomial equation has at least one solution. Archimedes found areas and volumes of many geometric figures. Newton developed the calculus. Euler solved the Königsberg bridge problem, the first problem in what is today called graph theory. Descartes developed coordinate geometry. Leonardo of Pisa worked with the sequence 1, 1, 2, 3, 5, 8, . . . , which bears his pseudonym (Fibonacci). Gödel proved (in 1930) that if there are an infinite number of objects (e.g., numbers or points) in a logical system, then no finite number of postulates about that system will enable all true statements in the system to be deduced from them. Russell showed (with Alfred North Whitehead) that all of mathematics can be traced back to fundamental ideas of logic. Cayley developed matrices. Pythagoras or his compatriots deduced the theorem bearing his name. Brahmagupta proved many theorems about quadrilaterals. Thales seems to have been the first to give a deductive proof of a theorem. Viète first introduced the idea of a variable as it is used in algebra. Riemann worked with a variety of non-Euclidean geometries. Von Neumann helped in the practical design of computers. Weyl contributed to quantum mechanics and many other areas.

Project 2

See Reference 4. There are also many books on the teaching of arithmetic that would be helpful.

Project 3

The Hindus were the first to use a numeral for zero and developed the numerals and arithmetic as we know it. Leonardo of Pisa was one of the first Europeans to work with our present number system. The Arabs transmitted the system to Europe because of their desire to spread the Moslem religion. From the seventh to the fifteenth century, Arabs (called Moors) lived in many of the towns of Spain and other places in southern Europe. The same year that Columbus sailed for America (1492), the Moors were banished from Spain. But during the centuries they had settled in Europe, they helped keep alive the mathematics that the Greeks and Hindus had developed.

Project 4

=, Robert Recorde, 1557
+, Johann Widmann, 1489
×, William Oughtred, 1631
÷, John Pell, 1631

−, Johann Widmann, 1489
√ , Christoff Rudolff, 1525
π, William Jones, 1706 (but usually attributed to Euler)

Before these symbols were invented, people used words or abbreviations to represent mathematical operations.

The Metric System

JANELLE A. ELROD

A POPULAR debate today centers on the use of the metric system of measurement in the United States. Supporters of the metric system point out that almost all the countries of the world now use it, and nonsupporters claim that the United States will never completely "Go Metric." You have probably noticed metric usage (such as kilometers and grams) more and more in daily activities because some U.S. companies and government agencies are now using the system.

To prepare you for a world that includes metrics, your textbooks have lessons on metric measurement. The purpose of your work in this unit is to help you to understand the metric system of measurement better and to learn about its history and development.

Projects

Project 1

Identify the seven metric base units, prefixes, and abbreviations. What names and prefixes are used for land measure? Which units of measure are most frequently used?

Guide: You are already familiar with some of the base units in the metric system (meter and gram) and with prefixes and abbreviations. You should concentrate on those units that are unfamiliar to you. When studying time, you may want to talk to someone in the military who can help you learn about the twenty-four-hour clock. Include the units for length, area, volume, capacity, and mass (weight) in your identification of the most commonly used units of measure. Look at References 4 and 5 for help and at arithmetic textbooks for review.

Project 2

Identify and explain each of the following: Gabriel Mouton; Système International d'Unités; Treaty of the Metre; Paris Academy of Sciences; International Conference of 1799; Metric Conversion Act of 1975; U.S. Metric Board; and SI.

Guide: References 2, 7, and 8 will help you with this identification. State what each has to do with the metric system. For example, ask yourself, "How does the Paris Academy of Sciences relate to the metric system of measurement?"

Project 3

The centimeter, meter, liter, milliliter, cubic centimeter, kilogram, and gram are frequently used units of measure. Identify two objects in your home, city, or state that use *each* of these units.

Guide: If you read the labels on cans and bottles and in newspapers or magazines, you will find examples of metric usage. Read the labels on containers for cold remedies and headache medicine. Metric terminology is also present in television advertisements. You may want to ask your parents and neighbors, business people, nurses, and doctors for other examples of metric usage.

Project 4

Make a list of ten companies or government agencies that use the metric system of measurement.

Guide: The people with whom you talked and the objects you listed for Project 3 are a starting point in identifying companies and agencies. References 6 and 9 also provide guidance.

Project 5

Determine the difference between base units and derived units. Explain the relationship of the base units of volume, capacity, and mass.

Guide: When completing Project 1, you discovered that *liter* is not a base unit. It is interesting to learn how the liter is related to the ideas of volume and mass (weight). This relationship is one that makes the metric system unique. Reference 3 is most useful for completing this requirement.

Project 6

Estimate and then measure two common items in each of the following categories: length, area, volume, capacity (liquid volume), mass (weight), and temperature. Record your estimate and your measurement.

Guide: The purpose of this activity is to help you to learn the "sizes" of objects using metric units. After several measurements, you should find that your estimates are improving. This activity will help you make accurate guesses when needed in the future and recognize the most appropriate unit to use when measuring. Here are some suggested items to estimate and then measure: a raisin, pecan, credit card, dollar bill, nickel, soft drink can, pitcher, sink, bedroom, and garage. You may want to measure some of these items in different ways. For example, you can measure a sink's capacity as well as its length, width, and depth.

Project 7

Complete two of the following activities:

- Use a metric recipe to prepare a favorite dish.
- Learn about engine sizes in motorcycles. How do these sizes relate to dirt and street bikes and motocross requirements?
- Arrange to show a film on the metric system to a group in your school or community.
- Identify three tools that have metric sizes and are used by mechanics.
- Draw a map of the area around your home. Identify the distance in kilometers between home and five places you frequently go.
- Obtain material on the metric system from five companies or industries and make a bulletin board display.

Guide: Look in grocery stores, on food boxes, and in foreign cookbooks, or write to national baking companies for recipes with metric measurements. Films can be found in your school media center or town library. Project 4 identifies companies that you can contact to request metric material. You may also request free materials from the Office of Metric Programs, Department of Commerce, Room 4082, 14th and Constitution Ave., N.W., Washington, D.C. 20230.

Further Investigations

1. Write to embassies of other countries for information on how they became metric. Of special interest might be the French embassy, because France has been a leader in the development of the metric system. All embassies are located in Washington, D.C.; your public library might have a Washington, D.C., telephone book from which you can get addresses.

2. How does the metric system relate to our base-ten number system and to U.S. currency. Discuss this relationship.

3. Write to companies that have gone metric. Find out why they converted, what the advantages are, and what difficulties they have faced.

4. By now you realize that the United States is slowly going metric—many companies and government agencies are already using the metric system. Even so, people debate about its use in everyday life. After looking at the advantages and disadvantages and what's happening today, decide if the U.S. should go metric. Reference 3 will help you with this question.

5. Devise a system of "metric measure" for one of the following: time (a ten-day week?); angles (100 degrees in a straight angle?); or space (light years?). Reference 1 might give you some ideas.

REFERENCES

1. Frasier, E. Lewis. "The Tenth Step—Metric Time and Angles." *Mathematics Teacher* 72 (April 1979): 248–53.
2. Hallerberg, Arthur E. "The Metric System: Past, Present—Future?" *Arithmetic Teacher* 20 (April 1973): 247–55.
3. Hallerberg, Arthur. "Commonly Listed Advantages of the Metric System." *Arithmetic Teacher* 20 (April 1973): 255.
4. Keller, J. J. and Associates. *Official Metric System Charts . . . Terms . . . Definitions . . . Clarified and Explained.* 145 W. Wisconsin Ave., Neenah, WI 54956. $1.00.
5. Leffin, Walter W. *Going Metric: Guidelines for the Mathematics Teacher.* Reston, Va.: National Council of Teachers of Mathematics, 1975.
6. National Bureau of Standards. "America Joins a Metric World." *Dimensions,* February 1976.
7. National Bureau of Standards. *A Metric America—a Decision Whose Time Has Come.* U.S. Metric Study, Special Publication 345. Washington, D.C.: Government Printing Office, 1971.
8. U.S. Metric Board. *America and the Metric System, A Capsule History.* Office of Metric Programs, Department of Commerce, Room 4082, 14th and Constitution Ave., N.W., Washington, D.C. 20230.
9. U.S. Metric Board. *Metric Usage Study: A Look at Six Case Histories.* Office of Metric Programs, Department of Commerce, Room 4082, 14th and Constitution Ave., N.W., Washington, D.C. 20230.

Teacher Notes

Project 1

The most frequently used units of measure are the kilometer, meter, decimeter, centimeter, square kilometer, square meter, square decimeter, square centimeter, cubic meter, cubic centimeter, kiloliter, kilogram, gram, and cubic decimeter.

Project 2

- Gabriel Mouton—a Frenchman who first suggested a decimal system of weights and measures using the meter as the basic unit of length.
- Système International d'Unités—the official name of the metric system as established by the Eleventh General Conference of Weights and Measures in 1960.
- Treaty of the Metre—established in 1875 by the United States and several other countries. These countries agreed that the world should adopt the metric system as the basic system of measurement.
- Paris Academy of Sciences—undertook an investigation to determine a uniform standard of weights and measures in the late 1700s. The study established the meter as the standard unit for length and derived basic units for volume and mass from it.
- International Conference of 1799—an international gathering convened in Paris for the formal presentation of the new metric system of measurement.
- Metric Conversion Act of 1975—declared a national policy of coordinating the increasing use of the metric system in the United States and established a seventeen-member U.S. Metric Board. This act meant that the United States would voluntarily convert to the metric system and that the costs of conversion would be absorbed by companies making the change.
- U.S. Metric Board—charged with coordinating and promoting all metric conversion activities in the U.S., but with no power to compel anyone to do anything. Composition of the board is specified by law to represent a broad spectrum of commerce, industry, education, labor, government, and other sectors of society.
- SI—the abbreviation for Système International d'Unités.

Project 5

The special relationships are the following:

1 cubic decimeter = 1 liter = 1 kilogram
1 cubic centimeter = 1 milliliter = 1 gram
1 cubic meter = 1 kiloliter = 1 metric ton

Mathematics and Home Economics

JANE F. SCHIELACK
CAROLYN KLEIN

HOME economics is the term that describes the knowledge and skills used in meeting individual and family needs in the home. Decisions about food and nutrition, clothing, housing, personal and family relationships, and time and money management are all parts of home economics. Mathematics plays an important role in home economics. One uses mathematics to measure, determine costs, and compare values when making decisions about food, clothing, and housing. Mathematics is also used to make visual aids like circle graphs for organizing and displaying information about managing time or money. Completing this unit will enable you to see how mathematics is used as a tool for collecting information and making decisions in a specific area of home economics that affects us all—food and nutrition.

Project 1

Define the word *Calorie*. Locate information about the number of Calories and the amounts of other nutrients recommended for males and females your age. Make a table to display this information.

Guide: References 1 and 2 are good sources for this information. If the publications cannot be found in your library, check with the home economics department in your school. Be aware that the Recommended Dietary Allowances (RDA) and the U.S. Recommended Daily Allowances (U.S. RDA) are not the same. You might be interested in comparing these recommendations in the table you design.

Limit your table to the nutrition information that is usually listed on food labels (e.g., protein, fat, carbohydrates, calcium, phosphorus, iron, vitamin A, vitamin C, thiamin, riboflavin, and niacin). Notice that the amounts are usually given in grams or milligrams.

Project 2

1. Keep a record for one day of all the food you eat. Using some source(s) of nutrition information, answer the following questions:

- How many Calories did you eat during this one day? What percentage of the recommended daily allowance does this figure represent?
- What percentage did you eat of the total recommended daily allowance for each category of nutrient in your table?
- What percentage of the Calories that you ate during the day was eaten for breakfast? Lunch? Supper? Snacks?
- Would you consider your eating habits during this one day to be fairly normal for you? Based on this consideration, would the average daily Calories you consume during one week probably be about the same, higher, or lower than the Calories consumed during this one day?

Guide: Carrying a small notepad with you during the day will help you remember to record each thing you eat. Information on nutrition can be found in References 3, 4, and 5, and in almanacs, or on the nutrition labels on food containers. Notice that the information given is usually for one serving. Be sure to consider the serving size when figuring the grams and milligrams of nutrients you have eaten. For example, the nutrition information on a small package of corn chips is for one serving, but the label says that the package contains two servings. If you have eaten the whole package of corn chips, that means twice the amount of nutrients listed on the package. If you use tables as in Reference 3 to calculate the nutrients, it will be necessary to estimate the amount of food eaten. A quick review of Reference 3 will show that

NCTM Projects to Enrich School Mathematics: Level 2

volume (e.g., milk), *weight* (e.g., hamburger), and *pieces* (e.g., apple) are the units of measurement used to describe serving size in this kind of table.

2. Plan a one-day menu for yourself that provides the recommended number of Calories and amounts of other nutrients.

Project 3

Using your one-day menu from Project 2, complete the following table and answer the questions.

Food	Packaged Amount	Amount Eaten	% = $\frac{\text{Amount Eaten}}{\text{Packaged Amount}}$	Package Price	Cost of Amount Eaten

1. What is the estimated cost of buying ingredients for this menu?

2. If this amount were your average daily food cost for nutritious meals, what would your food cost be each month?

3. A reasonable amount for one person to budget for food is 15 to 25 percent of his or her income. If you were planning to budget 18 percent of your monthly income for food costs, how much would you need to earn each month to afford the meals you planned for this project? (Assume that your monthly food cost is what you found in question 2.)

4. Do you think it necessary to have this monthly income in order to have nutritious meals?

Guide: Use References 2, 3, 4, and 5, or your home economics book. Many cookbooks also have information on nutrition.

Project 4

Assume that your school is planning some day camps this summer for students interested in working with microcomputers. The camp will be from 8:00 a.m. to 3:00 p.m. for five days. The school would like to provide lunches for the students if it is possible to provide nutritious ones for no more than $2 each. The enrollment for each camp is limited to fifteen students; some of the students' parents have volunteered to do whatever food preparation is necessary. With this information in mind, plan lunch menus for a week and display the cost and nutrition information in a way that would allow the school board to review it.

Guide: The lunch should provide about one-third of the students' daily nutritional requirements. The resources you used and the information you collected in the other projects should help with this one. Cookbooks and the food sections of some magazines and newspapers might give you ideas for interesting lunches.

When determining the allowable costs for the food, you might consider whether *each* lunch must be $2 or less or whether the five lunches can have an *average cost* of $2 or less.

You might want to consider using more than one chart or table to display the information about the lunches—for instance, one showing the food costs (either total cost or each lunch separately) and one showing the nutritional characteristics of the lunches. Remember that the information must convince the school board that the lunches are nutritious and within the budgeted amount.

REFERENCES

1. American Home Economics Association. *Handbook of Food Preparation.* 7th ed. Washington, D.C.: The Association, 1975.
2. National Academy of Sciences. *Recommended Dietary Allowances.* 9th ed. 1980.
3. U.S. Department of Agriculture. *Nutritive Value of Foods.* Home and Garden Bulletin 72. Washington, D.C.: Government Printing Office, 1981.
4. ———. *Nutrition Labeling—Tools for Its Use.* Agriculture Bulletin 382. Washington, D.C.: Government Printing Office, April 1975.
5. ———. *Nutritive Value of American Foods in Common Units.* Agriculture Handbook 456. Washington, D.C.: Government Printing Office, Nov. 1975.

The following cookbooks might be helpful:

Better Homes & Gardens All-Time Favorite series (bread, salad, meat, etc.)
Better Homes & Gardens Fix It Fast Cookbook
Better Homes & Gardens Homemade Cookies Cookbook
Better Homes & Gardens New Junior Cookbook
Better Homes & Gardens Complete Step-by-Step Cookbook
The Betty Crocker Cookbook
The New Boys' and Girls' Cookbook

Teacher Notes

Project 1

Recommended Daily Dietary Allowances (RDA)

(Designed for the maintenance of good nutrition of practically all healthy persons in the United States.)

Persons			Food energy	Protein	Minerals			Vitamin A	Thiamin	Ribo-flavin	Niacin	Ascorbic acid
Sex-age category	Age				Calcium	Phos-phorus	Iron					
	Years From	To	Calories	Grams	Milli-grams	Milli-grams	Milli-grams	Inter-national units	Milli-grams	Milli-grams	Milli-grams	Milli-grams
Males	11	14	2,700	45	1,200	1,200	18	5,000	1.4	1.6	18	50
	15	18	2,800	56	1,200	1,200	18	5,000	1.4	1.7	18	60
Females	11	14	2,200	46	1,200	1,200	18	4,000	1.1	1.3	15	50
	15	18	2,100	46	1,200	1,200	18	4,000	1.1	1.3	14	60

Adapted from a table published by the National Academy of Science.

Project 2

Students must be aware that the nutrition information given on food labels may not be consistent with the information in their chart from Project 1. If the food label gives the percentage of U.S. RDA and the chart is based on RDA, then the student should realize that more information is needed before comparisons can be made.

Stamps That Depict History and Mathematicians

MARTIN H. KESSLER

POSTAGE STAMPS for use in mailing letters and parcels have been in existence for less than 150 years. Sovereign governments print stamps of various denominations that, when affixed to an envelope, indicate that a fee has been paid for the delivery of the enclosed letter. In recent years, many countries have issued stamps of a topical and cultural nature. These stamps can be used for mailing, but they are especially attractive to stamp collectors, who are called *philatelists*.

The purpose of your work in this unit will be to acquaint you with some of the historical topics in mathematics and some of the mathematicians depicted on postage stamps of the world.

Projects

Project 1

List or collect a group of forty to fifty stamps, used or not, that have been issued by the United States, the United Nations, or foreign countries. These stamps must depict some historically mathematical development, mathematics study topic, equation, formula, design, or famous mathematician. At least 25 percent of your listing or collection should consist of stamps that honor famous mathematicians.

Guide: Reference 2 will greatly assist you in finding stamps that illustrate some of these particular topics, equations, early calculating machines, mathematical designs, or mathematicians. Reference 1 will give you an idea of the relative cost of such stamps. Prices are listed for both used (canceled) and mint (uncanceled) stamps.

Many local libraries stock at least one set of Scott stamp catalogs from the last five or six years. Also, local stamp dealers usually have a counter-top set available for customer use. In general, the cost of canceled stamps is much less than that of mint stamps.

Project 2

Write a short paragraph (75 to 100 words long) about each stamp or set of stamps that you have listed or collected in Project 1. Include the country of origin, date of issue, denomination of the stamp (especially if it's from a foreign country), and some brief background information on the topic or person depicted on the stamp.

Guide: Reference 1 will help you with some of the factual information that you may wish to include in your paragraph description. References 2 and 3 will help you with general topical information and biographical information about famous mathematicians.

Project 3

Mount and display in a binder or notebook the stamps that you have collected. Group the stamps alphabetically by topic or country of issue on lined or unlined paper.

Guide: Some of the stamps that you will find will be part of a set of two, three, or more stamps. You should display the entire set or partial set on the same page.

In mounting the stamps, you should use postage stamp hinges or any type of regular stamp mount, which are usually available from stamp and coin dealers at a minimal cost. Do *not* lick mint stamps and paste them on the mounting sheet. Also, do *not* use any type of glue, paste, tape, or other strong adhesive, since these will stain, discolor, and ultimately destroy the stamp.

REFERENCES

1. *Scott's Standard Postage Stamp Catalog.* New York: Scott Publishing Co., 1983.
2. Schaaf, William L. *Mathematics and Science: An Adventure in Postage Stamps.* Reston, Va.: National Council of Teachers of Mathematics, 1978.
3. Eves, Howard. *An Introduction to the History of Mathematics.* Rev. ed. New York: Holt, Rinehart & Winston, 1966.
4. Newman, James R. *The World of Mathematics.* Vols. 1–4. New York: Simon & Schuster, 1956.

Law of Pythagoras

Einstein's formula

Sonya Kovalevski

Photos from Mathematics and Science:
An Adventure in Postage Stamps,
By William L. Schaaf

Moon landing

Ptolemy

A pioneer of rocketry: Goddard

Teacher Notes

Much of the grading of the project will be concerned with how explicitly the student has followed the instructions.

You may want to arrange a date when it would be opportune for the student to make an oral presentation to your mathematics class. The presentation could include a summary of some of the written descriptions and a discussion of some of the interesting characteristics of a particular stamp or set of stamps.

Below is a list of some of the many stamps in the mathematical topical area that can be readily found and purchased at a nominal cost, for the most part. Some of these countries and stamp numbers could be given out to the student who develops a snag in finding enough stamps to complete the project.

Country, Scott Numbers

Ascension (Island)
140

Austria
B282, B315–316 (two of a set of semipostal issues)

Australia
531, 541–44 (set of four)

Belgium
877, 944

Brazil
687, 739, 815

Canada
396, 542, 737

Chile
277–80 (set of four)

Colombia
594, 742, C510 (air mail)

Denmark
300, 415, 463

Finland
373, 553, 612

France
306, 330, 331, 857, 861, 869, 871, 926, 1038, 1047, 1048, 1067, 1416, B181, B298 (expensive), B332, B384

Germany (West)
360, 725, 792, 962, 1104, 1123, 1246

DDR (East Germany)
58, 62, 63, 66, 338, 383–84, 811, 1501

Greece
835, 582–83, RA91 (revenue issue)

Great Britain
466

Haiti
577, 680–81, C121

Hungary
479, 1321, 1589, 1621–23, 2165, 2485

Iraq
390–92

Israel
117, 256–58

Mexico
C241

Netherlands
451, 487, B497–500

Nicaragua
877–81, C751, C761–65

Pakistan
281, 364

Poland
584–85, 882, 1178, 1659–61, 1915–18, 1956–60, B129

Romania
727–28, 756, 1345, 1876, 2405

Russia
838–40, 1098–99, 1570, 1575, 2009

Rwanda
84, 88

Spain
1159

Surinam
389–90, 421–23, B189

Switzerland
311, 549, 555, B303

Tanzania
225–28

United Nations
137–38, 223, 231, 238–39, C15.

United States
1011, 1109, 1201, 1237, 1258, 1260, 1274, 1285, 1314

NCTM Projects to Enrich School Mathematics: Level 2

Tangrams

EDNA F. BAZIK

THE seven-piece tangram puzzle originated in China, where it gained popularity in the early 1800s. One conjecture is that this puzzle evolved when a man named Tan dropped a square tile on the floor and it broke into seven pieces. (The name *tangram* means Tan's pictures.) The seven geometric pieces included one medium-sized triangle, two small triangles, two large triangles, one square, and one parallelogram. When Tan tried to put the pieces back together to form a square, he found that several other shapes and patterns emerged. Some of the many shapes that it was possible to make using all seven pieces included birds, sailboats, people, houses, and animals. Tan was so delighted with this new puzzle that he shared it with his friends, and they made their own sets from ivory, paper, or wood. Shortly, people all around the world were making tangrams. In *Tangrams, Picture-Making Puzzle Game,* Peter Van Note observes that during the nineteenth century the tangram puzzle became a craze of such notable people as John Quincy Adams, Edgar Allan Poe, Napoleon Bonaparte, and Lewis Carroll. All these people and others had fun with this seven-piece puzzle. Let's investigate how we can make a tangram and then involve ourselves with various activities using this clever puzzle!

Projects

Project 1

Research the available literature on tangrams by selecting references from those listed at the end of this unit. Write a 500-word essay on the history of the tangram.

1. Include the long history of the original tangram puzzle, the popularity of this puzzle, and how its name was derived. Give the details of how the tangram originated.

2. Identify how the puzzle's popularity craze moved throughout Asia, Europe, and the United States. Consider the historical as well as the mathematical aspects of the tangram.

3. Include the dimensions of the original Chinese ivory puzzle. Discuss the measure of all the angles in each of the seven pieces.

4. Interview children and adults to see if they have discovered the tangram puzzle. Be sure to talk with adults who are over seventy years of age, too!

Guide: Read References 6, 8, 13, 16, and 20, which are listed at the end of this unit. Check references that are available in your school library and the public library in your city. (Remember to check the encyclopedias.) Also, ask your teacher for any other possible resources.

Project 2

Make a tangram puzzle by *folding and cutting*. Follow this set of directions:

1. Cut out a 10 cm × 10 cm square.
2. Fold the paper twice to form two diagonal lines.
3. Cut along one of the diagonals to make two large triangles.
4. Cut along the fold of one of the large triangles. Label these resulting two pieces A and B and put them aside.
5. Using the large triangle, bring the tip of the right angle vertex to the center of the hypotenuse and fold.
6. Cut along this new fold. Label this resulting triangle C and put it aside.

7. Fold the remaining piece, which is a trapezoid, as shown below. Bring the left tip over to meet point A of the crease line and fold.
8. Cut along this new fold and label the triangle D. Put it aside.

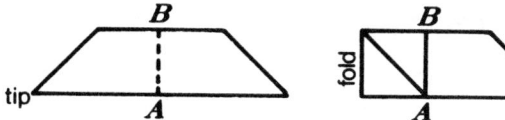 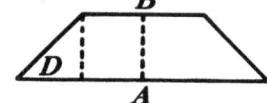

9. Cut the remaining piece along fold AB. Label the resulting square F and put it aside.

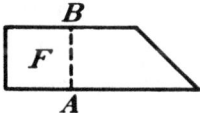

10. Use the last piece now. Bring tip A up to tip I and fold.

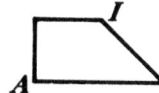 

11. Cut along fold BX. Label the triangle E and the parallelogram G as shown below.

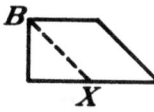 

You have now completed the tangram pieces by folding and cutting.

Project 3

Make a tangram puzzle by *geometric construction*. Follow this set of directions (from Reference 17):

1. Draw a diagonal segment ($\overline{AC}$) in the square below.
2. Label E and F the midpoints of $\overline{AB}$ and $\overline{BC}$, respectively. Draw $\overline{EF}$.
3. Label G the midpoint of $\overline{EF}$. Draw $\overline{GD}$.
4. Construct a line segment perpendicular to $\overline{AC}$ from point E.
5. Construct a line segment from point G to $\overline{AC}$, parallel to $\overline{BC}$.

On completion of these five steps, do you find that your resulting figure is the tangram?

Project 4

Relate the area of tangram pieces to percent.

Materials: Set of tangram pieces (seven-piece puzzle shown below)
10 × 10 square centimeter graph paper grid
Piece of cardboard
Scissors
Glue

Procedure: Cut out the large square of the total set of tangram pieces.
Do *not* cut the seven individual tangram pieces.
Glue this set of tangram pieces on a piece of cardboard.
On the reverse side of this piece of cardboard, glue a 10 × 10 piece of square centimeter graph paper grid.
Now cut out the seven individual tangram pieces.

Answer the following questions:

1. If each side of the large square is 10 centimeters, find the areas of A, B, C, D, E, F, and G. Record each of these area measurements in the table.
2. Find the total area of all seven tangram pieces.
3. Find what percent of the whole area each piece is. Record each of these percents in your table.

Set of Tangram Pieces

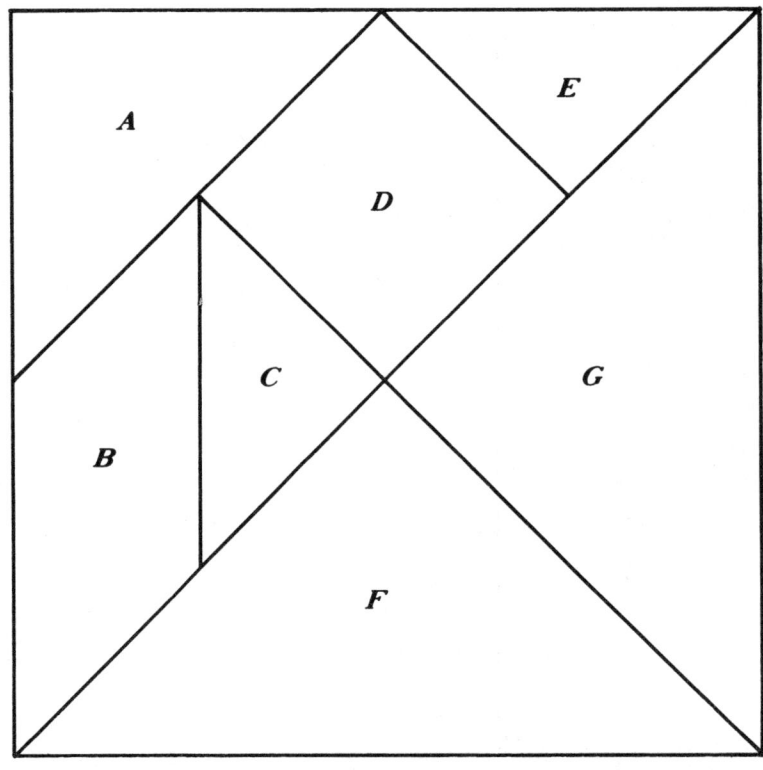

Tangram Piece	Area of Tangram Piece in cm²	Fractional Part of Tangram Piece in Relation to Total Set	Percent Each Tangram Piece Is of Whole Set
A			
B			
C			
D			
E			
F			
G			

Do the following activities from Reference 1:
1. If the area of C is 2 cm², then find the area of A, B, D, E, F, and G.
2. If the area of F is 3 cm², then find the area of A, B, C, D, E, and G.
3. What fractional part of D is E?
4. What fractional part of A is C?
5. What fractional part of B is C?

Project 5

Piece together tangram pieces.

Materials: Set of tangram pieces
Square centimeter graph paper
Pencil

1. Using a set of tangram pieces, try to make either a square, rectangle, triangle, parallelogram, or trapezoid by using any one tangram piece. Then, using a set of tangram pieces, try to make a square, rectangle, triangle, parallelogram, or trapezoid by using any two tangram pieces. Continue in this manner by using any three tangram pieces, then any four tangram pieces, . . . to any seven tangram pieces. Some are not possible. If your answer is yes, draw a sketch of the polygon in the chart on page 65. If it is not possible, write no in the chart.

2. Sketch each of the following exercises on graph paper after you have manipulated the tangram pieces into the appropriate figure.

   a) Put two or more tangram pieces together to form a shape that is congruent to another tangram piece.

   b) Use the two small triangle tangram pieces to make three different plane geometric figures.

   c) Make a pentagon using two tangram pieces.

   d) Make a hexagon using five tangram pieces.

   e) Using the five smaller tangram pieces, make a square. Place the two larger triangles around the square to form a triangle.

   f) Make a square using the five smaller tangram pieces. Place the two larger triangles around the square to form a parallelogram. Place the two larger triangles around the square to form a trapezoid.

g) Make each numeral (0, 1, 2, . . . 9) using all seven tangram pieces for each numeral.

h) Make every lowercase letter of the alphabet, using all seven tangram pieces. Can you make all of them?

i) Make convex polygons by using all seven tangram pieces. (Remember that a convex polygon is one in which all of its diagonals occur inside the polygon.) There are 12 different convex polygons: one is a triangle, five are quadrilaterals, two are pentagons, and four are hexagons. Can you find all twelve?

Tangram Pieces Used	Square	Rectangle (Not a Square)	Triangle	Parallelogram	Trapezoid
1					
2					
3					
4					
5					
6					
7					

Project 6

Investigate methods to find a line of symmetry in a polygon. Try each of the following methods:

a) Use a mirror or a Mira.
b) Fold a shape.
c) Flip a figure that is cut out.

Answer the following questions:

1. How many lines of symmetry can you find in the square of the tangram puzzle? Sketch your findings.
2. How many lines of symmetry can you find in the parallelogram of the tangram puzzle? Sketch your findings.
3. Use any two tangram pieces and try the following problems: (Remember to sketch each of your findings.)
    a) Make a quadrilateral that has no line of symmetry.
    b) Make a quadrilateral that has exactly four lines of symmetry.
    c) Make a quadrilateral that has exactly two lines of symmetry.
4. Use five tangram pieces and try to make a quadrilateral that has exactly four lines of symmetry.
5. Which of the seven tangram pieces have *turn symmetry*? (Use a reference or resource to check on the definition of the term *turn symmetry*.)

Guide: Read the sections entitled "Informal Geometry through Symmetry" and "Symmetry" in *Readings in Geometry from the "Arithmetic Teacher,"* pp. 32–38 (Reston, Va.: National Council of Teachers of Mathematics, 1970).

REFERENCES

1. Bazik, Edna, and Barbara Wilmot. *Mind Over Math*. Phoenix, Ariz.: Resources for the Gifted, 1980.
2. Bennett, Albert B., Jr., and Leonard T. Nelson. *Mathematics, an Activity Approach*. Boston, Mass.: Allyn & Bacon, 1979.
3. Bezuszka, Stanley, S.J. *Contemporary Motivated Mathematics*. Chestnut Hill, Mass.: Boston College Press, 1970.
4. Brownlee, Juanita. *Tangram Geometry in Metric*. Hayward, Calif.: Activity Resources Co., 1975.
5. Buell, Clayton E., Irvin Schwartz, and Alan Barson. *Activities with Tangrams*. Newton, Mass.: Selective Educational Equipment, 1978.
6. Dudeney, Henry E. *Amusements in Mathematics*. New York: Dover Publications, 1970.
7. Foster, Thomas E. *Tangram Patterns*. Palo Alto, Calif.: Creative Publications, 1977.
8. Gardner, Martin. *The 2nd Scientific American Book of Mathematical Puzzles and Diversions*. New York: Simon & Schuster, 1969.
9. Ginther, John L. *Math Experiments with the Tangram*. Pacific Grove, Calif.: Midwest Publications Co., 1972.
10. Jenkins, Lee, and Peggy McLean. *It's a Tangram World*. San Leandro, Calif.: Educational Science Consultants, 1972.
11. Johnston, Susan. *The Fun with Tangrams Kit*. New York: Dover Publications, 1977.
12. Kelley, S. Jeanne. *Learning Mathematics through Activities*. Cupertino, Calif.: James E. Freel & Associates, 1973.
13. Loyd, Sam. *The 8th Book of Tan*. New York: Dover Publications, 1968.
14. McLaughlin, Jack. *The Tangram*. Englewood Cliffs, N.J.: Prentice-Hall, 1976.
15. Morris, Janet. *Investigations in Mathematics*. Monograph no. 13. Lansing, Mich.: Michigan Council of Teachers of Mathematics, 1979.
16. Read, Ronald C. *Tangrams, 330 Puzzles*. New York: Dover Publications, 1965.
17. Schadler, Reuben A., and Dale G. Seymour. *Pic-A-Puzzle*. Palo Alto, Calif.: Creative Publications, 1970.
18. Seymour, Dale. *Tangramath*. Palo Alto, Calif.: Creative Publications, 1971.
19. Sobel, Max A., and Evan M. Maletsky. *Teaching Mathematics: A Sourcebook of Aids, Activities, and Strategies*. Englewood Cliffs, N.J.: Prentice-Hall, 1975.
20. Van Note, Peter. *Tangrams, Picture-Making Puzzle Game*. Rutland, Vt., & Tokyo: Charles E. Tuttle Co., 1966.

Teacher Notes

Project 3

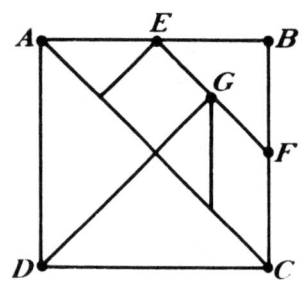

Project 4 Total area of all seven pieces is 100 cm².

Tangram Piece	Area in cm²	Fractional Part Area Is of Total Set	Percent Area Is of Total Set
A	12 1/2	1/8	12 1/2%
B	12 1/2	1/8	12 1/2%
C	6 1/4	1/16	6 1/4%
D	12 1/2	1/8	12 1/2%
E	6 1/4	1/16	6 1/4%
F	25	1/4	25%
G	25	1/4	25%

Further activities, Project 4

1. A, B, D = 4 cm²;
   E = 2 cm²;
   F, G = 8 cm²

2. A, B, D = 1.5 cm²;
   C, E = 0.75 cm²;
   G = 3 cm²

3. 1/2
4. 2/1
5. 2/1

Project 5.1

No. of Pieces	Square	Rectangle (Not Square)	Triangle	Parallelogram	Trapezoid
1	▢	NO	△	▱	NO
2	◩	NO	△	▱	▱
3	NO	▭	△	▱	▱
4	◩	▭	△	▱	▱
5	◩	▭	△	▱	▱
6	NO	▭	NO	NO	▱
7	◩	▭	△	▱	▱

48 NCTM Projects to Enrich School Mathematics: Level 2

Project 5.2

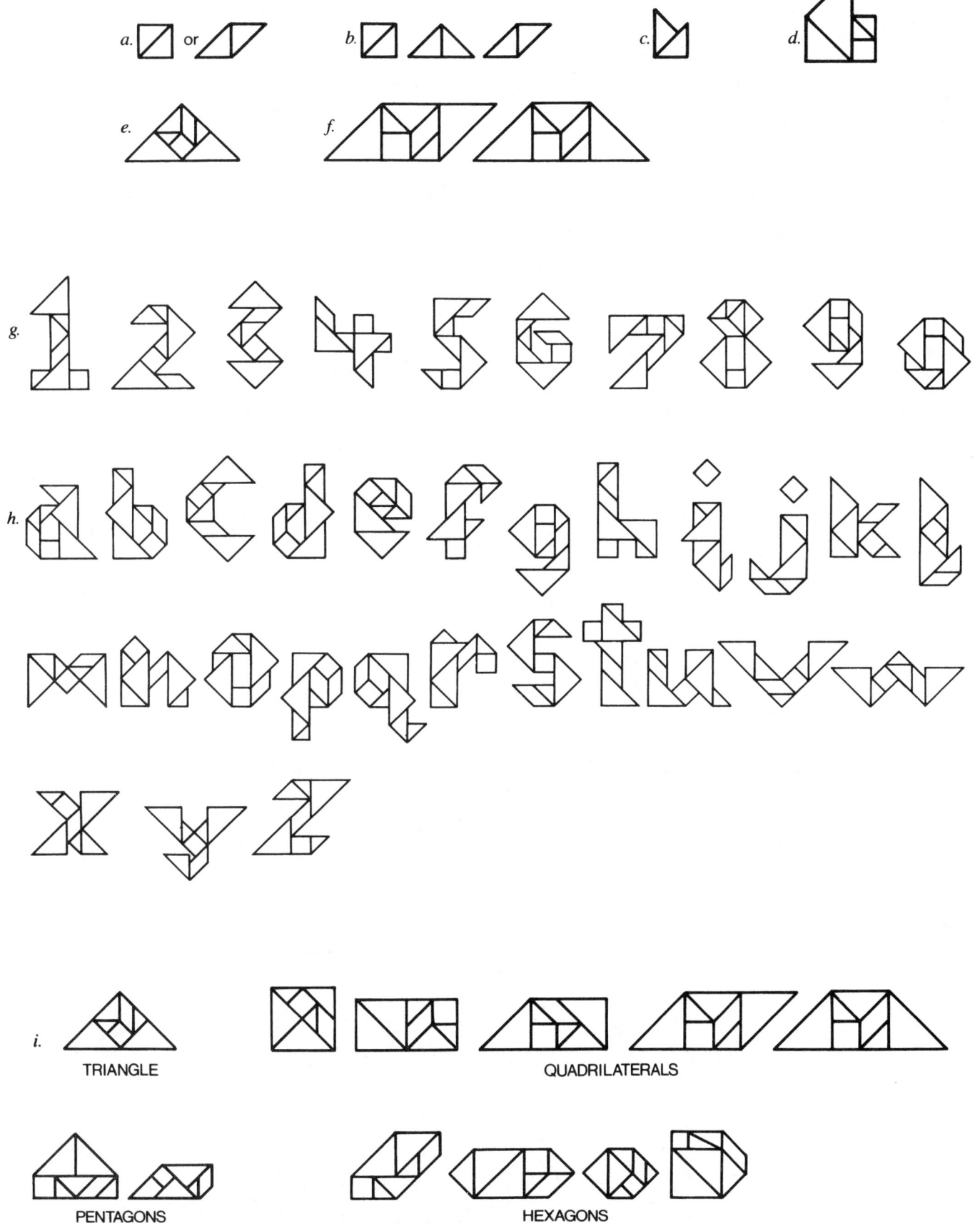

NCTM Projects to Enrich School Mathematics: Level 2

49

Project 6

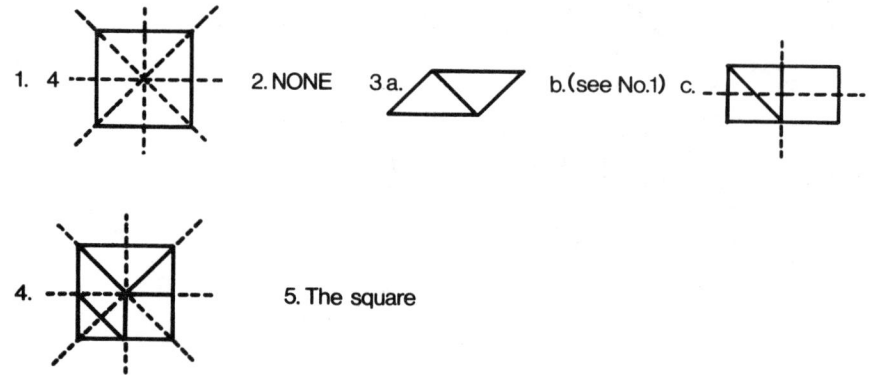

4. 5. The square

Applications of Mathematics in Nursing

LLOYD I. RICHARDSON
JUDITH KNIGHT RICHARDSON

MATHEMATICS is used daily by most people in all professions, but it is especially used by nurses in the performance of professional activities. If you have given thought to a career in nursing, you might be curious about how mathematics is used in this profession.

On a daily basis, nurses are required to perform tasks and procedures that involve some method of measurement, simple graphing, recording data, and actual mathematical calculations. Nurses must know and use the metric, apothecaries', and household systems of measure. The recording of patients' vital signs (i.e., temperature, pulse, respiration, and blood pressure) is performed frequently. Calculations may be necessary to determine the number of tablets or capsules a patient needs and are routine in all patient care settings. Nurses often calculate medications for intramuscular injections or fluids for intravenous administration. Intramuscular injections are often referred to as *shots* and intravenous medications are often referred to as *IVs* or in-the-vein medications (they come in bottles or bags hung by the patient's bed). There is no margin for error in these calculations because a person's safety and welfare could be at risk.

As you can readily determine from the examples mentioned above, mathematics is an applied science as it relates to the nursing profession. More specific examples of how mathematics is applied in nursing will be examined in the required sections that follow. It can be very exciting to discover the usefulness of mathematics in a profession such as nursing.

Projects

Project 1 (Systems of Measurement)

Review and use the following systems of measures:

1. Metric system
2. Apothecaries' system

Guide: Read and work through the instructional section that follows.

The nurse uses two basic systems of weights and measures when involved with medications for patients. These two systems are the apothecaries' system and the metric system. The primary system used is the metric system; however, the apothecaries' system is extremely valuable and still used extensively.

The Metric System

Using one of the references at the end of the unit, review the metric system. Then answer the questions in exercise 1.1.

Exercise 1.1

Using references 1, 2, or 3 at the end of the unit, look up the metric system and answer these questions:

1. What is the unit of measure and abbreviation for —
   a) unit of volume (capacity)?
   b) unit of weight (mass)?
   c) unit of length?
2. What are the six most common prefixes and their abbreviations?

3. Along with the numerical data, provide the abbreviation if the name is given.
   a) 27 millimeters = _____ mm
   b) 4 cl = _____ centiliters
   c) 25 centigrams = 25 _____
   d) 17 meters = _____
   e) 1.35 milliliters = _____
   f) 209 dg = _____
   g) 5 cm = _____
   h) 1487 mg = _____
   i) 43 dal = _____

4. Complete each of the following:
   a) 1 liter = _____ deciliters = _____ milliliters
   b) 1 kiloliter = _____ liters = _____ ml
   c) 1 gram = _____ kg = _____ mg

5. Is there a relationship between 1 cubic centimeter of fluid (called 1 cc) and 1 milliliter of the same fluid? Explain your answer.

The Apothecaries' System

Although the metric system will inevitably replace the apothecaries' system, the latter is still used today by physicians and nurses and will continue to be used for the next few decades. Therefore, the nurse must understand both the apothecaries' and metric systems.

In the apothecaries' system the basic unit for weight is the *grain*. When the system was established, the dry weight unit, the grain, was the weight of a grain of wheat. The abbreviation for grain is gr.

The *dram* is the next larger unit. A dram is 60 grains. The symbol for a dram can be thought of as a z with a tail: ʒ . After the dram, the *ounce* is the next larger unit in the apothecaries' system. An ounce equals 8 drams. The symbol for an ounce is ℥ . Thus

$$1℥ = 8ʒ .$$

(This symbol, ℥ , can be thought of as a greater than symbol, >, attached to the symbol for dram.) The next larger unit is the pound (lb.), which equals 12 ounces.

In the apothecaries' system, both roman numerals and Hindu-Arabic numerals are used in writing measurements. When the name is spelled out, Hindu-Arabic numerals are used to express the number value:

$$3 \text{ drams}$$

When the symbol (abbreviation) for the unit is used, roman numerals may be used to express the number value:

$$ʒ \text{ iii}$$

When roman numerals are used, they always follow the unit symbol. Lowercase letters (for example, i, v, x) are used in writing numbers in the apothecaries' system. Therefore,

$$1 \text{ ounce} = 8 \text{ drams}$$

can be written

$$℥i = ʒ \text{ viii.}$$

Frequently, large numbers (50 and over) are expressed using Hindu-Arabic numerals. Fractions are always written using Hindu-Arabic numerals, for example, $gr\frac{1}{8}$, $gr\frac{1}{4}$, $gr\frac{1}{16}$. The fraction $\frac{1}{2}$ occurs so often that a special symbol is used. The Latin word for one-half is semis, abbreviated ss: $7\frac{1}{2}$ grains = fr viiss.

52   NCTM Projects to Enrich School Mathematics: Level 2

Exercise 1.2

What does each abbreviation mean?

1. gr viii = 7 grains
2. ℨ ix = _____
3. ℥ v = _____
4. gr iss = _____
5. gr $\frac{1}{4}$ = _____

The *minim* (♏) is the unit of volume in the apothecaries' system. A minim is defined as the quantity of water weighing the same as 1 grain of wheat.

In the apothecaries' system the next largest unit of volume is the fluidram (fℨ): 1 fluidram is 60 minims

$$1 \text{ fluidram} = 60 \text{ minims or } f\text{ℨ } i = 60 ♏$$

After the fluidram, the next largest unit is the fluidounce (f℥): 1 fluidounce (f℥) equals 8 fluidrams. Thus:

$$f℥\ i = f\text{ℨ}\ viii$$

The nurse must be aware of some special terminology and abbreviations that are not encountered in the everyday lives of people.

Your assignment is to attempt to find the following terms and abbreviations in the library. You might consult a medical library if one is available. Should your library not contain the references provided, plan to ask the nurse the meaning of the words and abbreviations during the interview in Project 2.

Exercise 1.3

Find the definition or abbreviation for the following:

grain— _____   prn— _____

dram— _____   ss— _____

gtt— _____   tid— _____

minim— _____

Project 2

Interview a registered nurse (RN) and write a report of the interview.

Guide: The assignment sheet that follows this guide will provide a vehicle for you to record information from the interview so that it will be easily accessible for the report. You might wish to use a tape recorder so that you can listen to the tape to be certain you didn't miss an important fact, since it is often hard to record data as fast as the discussion progresses.

During the interview, inquire about the type of degree the nurse received and the mathematics courses needed for the degree. It is more important to determine the types of topics in the courses than it is to get their titles (such as College Algebra). Have the nurse identify five or more ways mathematics (or arithmetic) is used on a daily basis. These could include some items the nurse records numerically or some examples of actual mathematical computations. If the nurse cites examples of blood pressure or temperature measurement, ask what the normal ranges of these measurements are and what would be done when they are outside the normal range.

The assignment sheet is a skeletal guide of questions you will want to ask. However, if the nurse comments on something that interests you but is not on the form, by all means follow up with questions about it. You might want to show the nurse your assignment sheet so that she or he will know what you will be talking about.

Assignment (Project 2)

Use this form as a guide for the interview, but follow up on any subjects that interest you even if they are not included on this form.

Name (optional)_____

Year graduated_____ Degree_____

Degree received from_____

Mathematics courses taken:

Five ways mathematics is used by the nurse:

Comments:

Project 3

Using a medicine cup and syringe

Guide: To complete this project, you should complete the instructional phase and be able to indicate the amount of solution to be administered. To administer medication to patients, the nurse uses a medicine cup or a syringe. The medicine cup has two scales of measure pictured on one side. These two scales are from the metric and apothecaries' systems. Pictured in figure 1 is a medicine cup that has been shaded to simulate that 5 ml of fluid is in it.

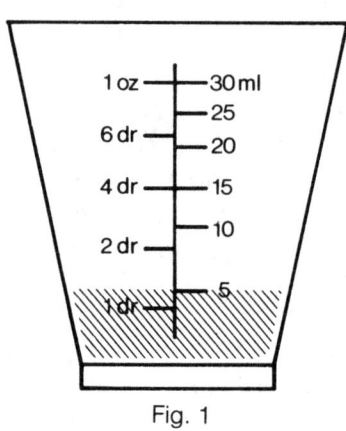

Fig. 1

Exercise 3.1

1. Shade the cups to indicate the desired amount of fluid in each.

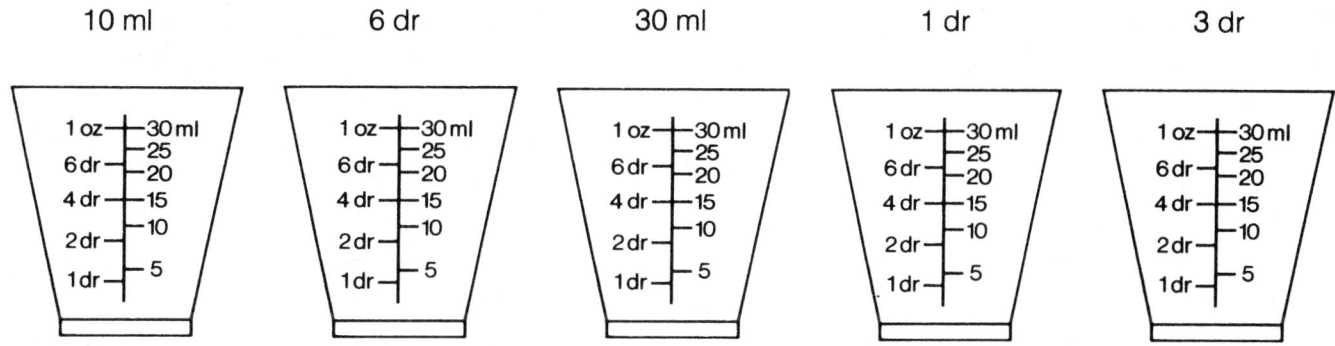

2. Find a measure on the apothecaries' scale that is approximately equivalent to a measure on the metric scale. What can you determine from this?
3. Regarding the metric scale, why is the distance from 5 ml to 10 ml so much more than the distance from 25 ml to 30 ml?

When the medication measure must be very precise, the medicine cup would be inappropriate. The syringe is used when precise measure is required. Pictured in figure 2 is a typical syringe used by the nurse when administering medications.

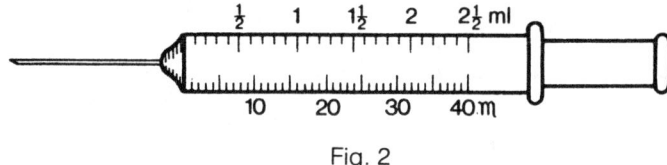

Fig. 2

You will notice that once again there are two scale of measure; however, each mark on the metric scale is one-tenth of a milliliter, thus allowing very precise measurement. You will also notice that the apothecaries' scale is in terms of minims (ℳ). Spend a few minutes reviewing the apothecaries' system studied in Project 1. Pay particular attention to the minim measure.

Exercise 3.2

1. Shade each syringe to simulate the desired amount of fluid.

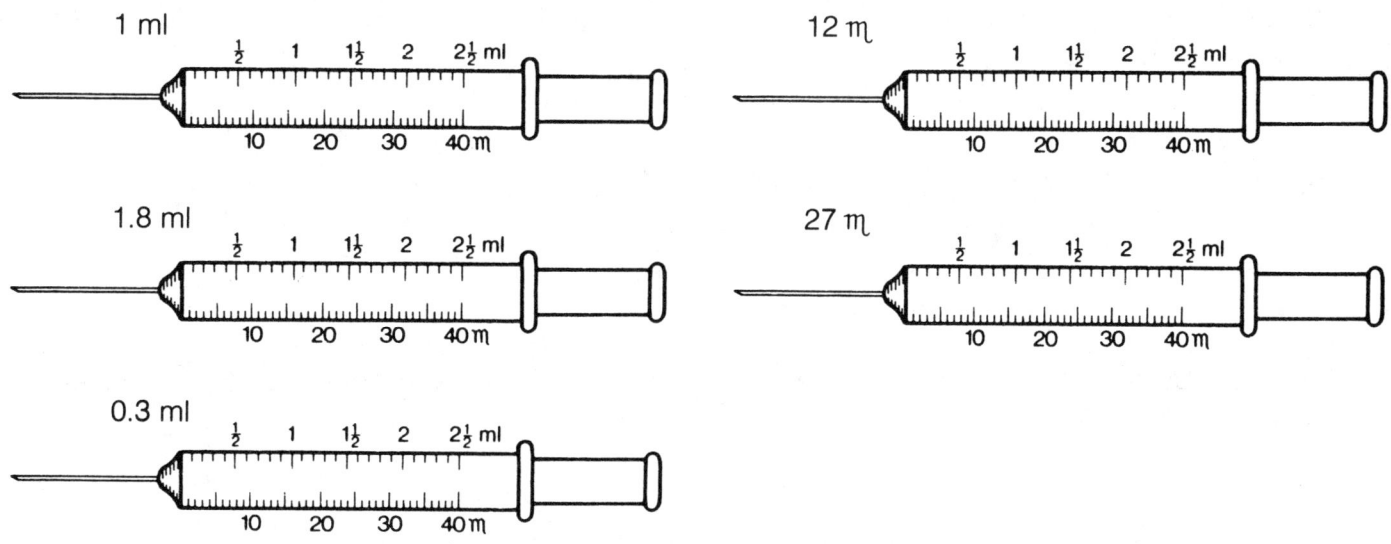

2. Is it the same distance from 0.5 ml to 1 ml as it is from 2 ml to 2.5 ml? Why or why not?

NCTM Projects to Enrich School Mathematics: Level 2

Project 4

Visit a pharmacy and interview a pharmacist. Write a report of the visit and the interview.

Guide: The assignment sheet is designed to aid you in both the visit to the pharmacy and the interview with the pharmacist. You should call the pharmacy and make an appointment with the pharmacist. Be sure to arrive about ten minutes early so you will be available when the pharmacist is free. The visit includes two components: the pharmacist interview and looking at some of the nonprescription medications available on the shelves.

With the pharmacist

Ask the pharmacist to show you a common medicine, an antibiotic perhaps, that is dispensed in both tablet (or capsule) and liquid form. Ask him or her to point out the strength of the medicine. *Strength* is determined by the number of milligrams per tablet, teaspoon, or milliliter. Ask to be shown a medication dispensed in *grams*. Pay special attention to the way the label is marked and ask the pharmacist to explain the markings if you do not understand them.

Ask the pharmacist for examples of a medicine that necessitates giving special instructions to the client. What are those instructions and why are they necessary?

Have the pharmacist show you different medicines so that you can see how the measurement units (such as gram, milligram, grain, etc.) are abbreviated.

On the shelves

Now browse around the pharmacy and find a medicine available in three strengths (these may be the same medicine from three different companies).

Assignment (Project 4)

Use this form as a guide for questions during the pharmacy visit.

1. Pharmacy name:

2. Medicine dispensed in both tablet/capsule and liquid form. List strengths.

3. List name and strength of a drug dispensed in *grains.*

4. Example of a medicine requiring special instructions to the client. List medicine, strength, and special instructions.

5. Examples of different medicines with measurement unit abbreviations:

6. Find two different medicines that come in three different strengths. List the medicine and the strengths for each.

Project 5

Calculate standard medication problems encountered by the nurse when administering drug medications.

Guide: The nurse often encounters a medication order that requires a dosage different from the way the drug is packaged. This requires that the nurse use mathematical computations to determine the correct amount to administer. For instance, the doctor orders 60 mg of codeine for a patient, J. Doe. The codeine tablets in the narcotic cabinet are labeled codeine 30 mg. Thus,

the desired dosage is 60 mg;

the on-hand is 30 mg per tablet.

There are two ways to calculate the correct amount to administer. The first way is to use proportions. If you have not studied proportions, go to the second method of solution.

To use proportions, set up two ratios. The on-hand codeine is:

$$\frac{30 \text{ mg}}{1 \text{ tablet}}$$

The desired codeine is:

$$\frac{60 \text{ mg}}{n \text{ tablets}}$$

n is used to represent the number of tablets needed. Setting the two ratios equal yields this proportion:

$$\underset{\text{on hand}}{\frac{30 \text{ mg}}{1 \text{ tablet}}} = \underset{\text{desired}}{\frac{60 \text{ mg}}{n \text{ tablets}}}$$

Solving,

$$\frac{30}{1} = \frac{60}{n}$$

$$30n = 60(1)$$

$$30n = 60$$

$$n = \frac{60}{30} = 2$$

The correct number of tablets is 2. Secondly, we could reason that

1 tablet contains 30 mg

so

2 tablets contain 60 mg.

Let's work another example. The order is for ampicillin suspension 500 mg. The drug on hand is labeled

Ampicillin suspension
250 mg/5 ml

Using the proportion method to solve the problem, first set up the ratios:

$$\underset{\text{on hand}}{\frac{250 \text{ mg}}{5 \text{ ml}}} \quad \underset{\text{desired}}{\frac{500 \text{ mg}}{n \text{ ml}}}$$

Now solve by setting the ratios equal:

$$\frac{250}{5} = \frac{500}{n}$$

$$250n = 5(500)$$

$$250n = 2500$$

$$n = \frac{2500}{250} = 10$$

NCTM Projects to Enrich School Mathematics: Level 2

Administer 10 ml. Solving the problem by reasoning, we would have

250 mg in 5 ml,

so

500 mg in 10 ml.

Now shading the medicine cup to the correct level, we'll have

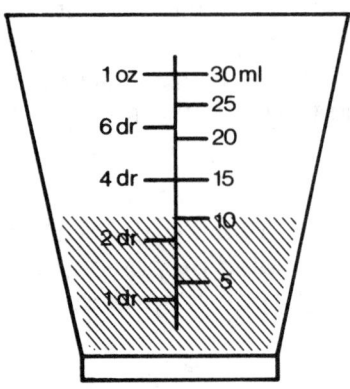

Exercise 5.1

Determine the correct dosage for each problem, then shade the medicine cup or syringe to simulate the amount to administer.

1. The physician ordered Demerol 15 mg intramuscular. The drug label reads Demerol 50 mg per 1 ml. How many milliliters does the patient receive?

2. The physician ordered Nembutal elixir 60 mg oral. The drug label reads Nembutal elixir 20 mg per 5 ml. How many milliliters does the patient receive?

   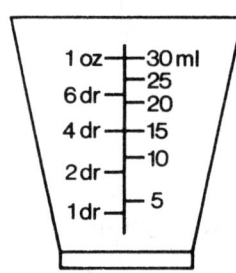

3. The order is for morphine 8 mg intramuscular. The drug label reads morphine 10 mg/ml. How many milliliters does the patient receive?

4. The order is for Feosol elixir 330 mg. The drug label reads Feosol elixir 220 mg/5 ml. How many milliliters does the patient receive?

Project 6

Calculate pediatric medications using rules often employed by the nurse.

Guide: Some hospitals have special divisions for infants and children; others integrate the infants and children throughout the hospital. It is important that the nurse who is caring for children know the safe range of dosages and that the amount of medication required for children is smaller than for adults. The physician always prescribes the medication, but the nurse must be aware of the usual dosage for frequently administered medications. Thus, the nurse often employs the following rules to check the prescription when there is some question on the nurse's part.

Young's rule (1 or 2 years to 12 years of age):

$$\text{Child's dose} = \frac{\text{child's age in years}}{\text{child's age in years} + 12} \times \text{adult dose}$$

Fried's rule (birth to 1 or 2 years of age):

$$\text{Infant's dose} = \frac{\text{age in months}}{150} \times \text{adult dose}$$

Clark's rule (birth to 12 years of age):

$$\text{Child's dose} = \frac{\text{weight of child in pounds}}{150 \text{ pounds}} \times \text{adult dose}$$

There are other rules, but they are too technical for our purposes here and require special equipment in order to use.

Exercise 6.1

Use each of the three rules to complete the medication.

1. The adult dose for aspirin is 10 grains. How many grains should be given to a 2-year-old child that weighs 20 lbs?
2. The adult dose for Demerol is 75 mg. How much Demerol should a 14-pound, 20-month-old infant receive?
3. The adult dose for Streptomycin is 500 mg. How much Streptomycin should a 30-month-old, 27-pound child receive?

REFERENCES

1. *Encyclopedia Americana*, 1983 ed., s.v. "Measures and Measuring Systems."
2. *Encyclopaedia Britannica*, 15th ed., s.v. "Weights and Measures."
3. *The New Book of Knowledge*, s.v. "Weights and Measures." New York: Grolier, 1982.
4. Richardson, Lloyd I., and Judith K. Richardson. *The Mathematics of Drugs and Solutions with Clinical Applications.* 2d ed. New York: McGraw-Hill, 1980.

Teacher Notes

The mathematics applications in nursing should be a unit of high interest to students because it provides justification for including measurement, fractions, roman numerals, ratios, and proportions in the mathematics curriculum.

We have endeavored to encourage students to use resource people in the community as well as to provide regular lesson requirements. One general note before addressing each project individually: If a number of students are completing this unit, encourage them to work together on Projects 2 and 4. These projects involve interviewing a nurse and a pharmacist, and we feel that a small group of students could work together so that there would be a minimum of disruption for the professional involved.

You should encourage students to look up unfamiliar words in the dictionary.

Project 1

We feel that this is one of the most difficult lessons because it involves the study of two systems of measure with which the student may not be familiar. This project is essential, however, in order for the student to gain the most benefit from Project 2. Due to the difficulty in the student finding a reference for the apothecaries' system, we have attempted to provide all the instruction necessary and to make this project self-contained. One of the best references is the *World Book Encyclopedia*. However, if a medical library is available in the community, encourage the student to use a nursing pharmacology text as a resource. Libraries vary so much regarding available sources in this area that we suggest the student work with the librarians to obtain a reference.

Exercise 1.1

1. a) liter, l—in nursing a lowercase L
   b) gram, g—in nursing a lowercase G
   c) meter, m—in nursing a lowercase M

2. kilo, k; hecto, h; deka, da; deci, d; centi, c; milli, m

3. a) 27 mm
   b) 4 centiliters
   c) 25 cl
   d) 17 m
   e) 1.35 ml
   f) 209 decigrams
   g) 5 centimeters
   h) 1487 milligrams
   i) 43 dekaliters

4. a) 1 liter = 10 dl = 1000 ml
   b) 1 kl = 1000 liters = 1 000 000 ml
   c) 1 gram = 0.001 kg = 1000 mg

5. 1 cc of fluid is exactly 1 ml of the fluid. Since 1000 cc is 1 liter and 1 liter is 1000 ml, then 1000 cc = 1000 ml. Thus, 1 cc = 1 ml. The use of cc instead of ml for the designation of fluid measures was universal until about 1975.

Exercise 1.2

2) 9 drams 3) 5 ounces 4) 1½ grains 5) ¼ grain

Exercise 1.3

grain: gr, the weight of one grain of wheat

dram: dr or ʒ, equals 60 grains

minim: ♏, unit of volume defined as quantity of water weighing one grain

prn: whenever necessary or needed

ss: one-half, semis

tid: three times per day

Project 2

A special form was developed to help students organize the questions they will wish to ask the nurse. You should evaluate the written reports to determine satisfactory completion of this project.

Project 3

Use of the medicine cup and syringe provides a simulation of how mathematical computations are used in a clinical situation. These will be used later when medication computations are performed.

Exercise 3.1

1) See that the student shades the cup to the appropriate level.
2) 4 drams is approximately equal to 15 (or 16) ml. Thus, 1 dram is about 4 ml. Nurses routinely know and use these facts.
3) This is to ensure that the student realizes that the slanted sides of the medicine cup yield more volume per unit of distance as one moves toward the top of the cup.

Exercise 3.2

1) See that the syringes are shaded to the correct position.
2) Since the cylinder is of uniform size, it is the same distance and contains the same amount of volume.

Project 4

After reading the student guide for Project 4, talk with the students about the visit and help them develop a plan. Be sure they know what the colloquial term *strength* means. Be sure to encourage small groups to make an appointment together, if possible. The form should serve as a guide for the students.

Project 5

Be aware that students will need to use proportions to solve these problems. For students not knowing proportions, the problems have been chosen so that the answers can be reasoned without much difficulty. Once the answer has been computed, the syringe or medicine cup should be shaded to simulate the amount of medication.

Exercise 5.1

1) 0.3 ml   2) 15 ml   3) 0.8 ml   4) 7.5 ml

Project 6

This project is designed to help students understand some of the procedures used by the nurse. The problems should also show that different formulas give different medication values.

These problems provide an excellent opportunity to discuss with the students why Clark's rule is the most accurate of the three rules presented. Body weight is the most accurate method of determining dosage because two children of the same age may have very different body weights. Using age in months or years gives a less accurate indication of the amount of drug needed by a child because these rules do not allow for individual differences in weight.

Exercise 6.1

1) 1.43 grains (Young's), 1.6 grains (Fried's), 1.33 grains (Clark's)
2) 9.1 mg (Young's), 10 mg (Fried's), 7 mg (Clark's)
3) 86.2 mg (Young's), 100 mg (Fried's), 100 mg (Clark's)

Exploring Angles

JOEL SCHNEIDER

GEOMETRY has been an important part of learning for more than two thousand years. As a student, you are continuing in a long tradition. In this unit you will have two types of work: reading to understand new ideas and drawing pictures to illustrate the ideas and solve problems.

Reading mathematics is not like reading a story or a play. Don't be surprised if you need to read a mathematics paragraph several times to understand its ideas. We all need to do that. Begin a section by reading and rereading the material several times. Working at the exercises will also help you to understand the ideas. When you come to an exercise, try the drawings. If you have difficulty (and you will have some, otherwise there would be little for you to learn here), do some rereading, then sketch and experiment with the drawings. Do not go past an exercise without spending sufficient time to solve the problems and draw all the pictures. Don't feel frustrated if you do not understand every idea or solve every problem immediately.

When you have finished an exercise, you will want to make final drawings that are neat and well organized and that clearly convey your solutions. One test of your work could be to see if a friend can understand what your drawings are meant to show. In the end we will suggest that you make a display to illustrate some of the ideas you have studied.

You will need the following materials:

- large, unlined paper (11" × 17", if possible)
- tracing paper
- sharp pencils (not too soft—#2½ or #3)
- a good eraser (no smudging)
- a red pencil and a blue pencil (both sharp!)
- a straightedge (a ruler is okay, but do you know the difference?)

Projects

Project 1

We study geometry to compare shapes systematically. To study a shape, we often look at its parts to see how they fit together. Your object will be to explore ways in which angles are a part of certain shapes. Before we look at angles, or even say what they are, we need to learn a few geometric ideas. All geometry starts with *points* and *lines*. When we do geometry, we draw pictures to help our thinking. We usually picture a line by drawing a stroke (no freehand drawing; use your straightedge, please). Since we think lines go on and on in two directions (to infinity, but that's another project), whatever we draw shows only a piece of the line and indicates the rest. We'll use arrowheads to indicate going on and on (fig. 1).

Fig. 1

We usually picture a point by drawing a dot. Since we think of points as being so small as to have no size (another approach to infinity), the size of a dot we draw is only important when we need to use several dots to make a more elaborate drawing (fig. 2). You probably tried your hand at follow-the-dots puzzles a long time ago. (If you don't remember, check with a young friend between six and eight years of age.) In such a puzzle, several dots are numbered. You start at dot 1, then draw a stroke to dot 2, followed by a stroke to dot 3, and so on. When solving these puzzles, most people sketch the strokes. Let's agree to use a straightedge in similar situations, then we will always draw pieces of lines.

Fig. 2

All this is included to tell you what the sizes of dots for points has to do with our work. Suppose the dots in a follow-the-dots puzzle are big compared to the thickness of our pencil lines. There are many ways we could connect the dots. But if the dots are small, we don't have much choice, at least so far as we can see (infinity again). See figure 3. Therefore, we ask you to take this pledge:

Pledge: I will be neat, draw dots that are small, and use a straightedge to connect them.

Fig. 3

By the way, for being careful, we gain something extra. If we draw two dots and connect them, we could keep on going and indicate a line. With carefully drawn dots, we can feel certain that anyone else connecting the dots will indicate the same line (fig. 4). This is an important idea that you will meet again in your future work with geometry.

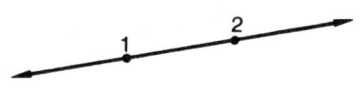

Fig. 4

We will call two points and the piece of line which connects them a *line segment*. We started with two points, connected them to form a line segment, then extended it in two directions to draw a line. We can reverse the steps by starting with a line, picking two points on it, and then erasing the parts of the line outside the line segment (fig. 5). Either way, the two points are called the *endpoints* of the line segment. There are many pairs of points to choose on a line, with each pair giving a line segment.

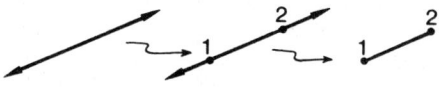

Fig. 5

Look at the line in figure 6. Four points are marked with *A, B, C,* and *D.* (We usually use letters rather than numbers to name points.) Each pair of these points gives us a line segment.

Now it's time to do some drawing. You will need paper; tracing paper; black, red, and blue pencils; and a straightedge. Remember to be neat and precise in your final drawings, even if you use scratch paper to sketch ideas.

NCTM Projects to Enrich School Mathematics: Level 2

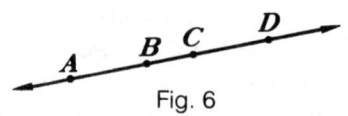

Fig. 6

Exercise 1. Make a drawing of a line similar to figure 6. Then make several copies, all on the same piece of paper. Pick two of the points A, B, C, or D. Circle their labels in red on the first copy of your line, then use a red pencil to draw the line segment connecting those points on the first copy. Pick another pair for the second copy. Continue until you cannot find another pair to pick. Make as many copies of the line as you need.

Exercise 2. Make another copy of your line. Pick one pair of points, circle their labels in red and draw their line segment in red (fig. 7). The picture should now look like one you have already drawn. Pick two more points, but circle them in blue and draw their segment in blue (fig. 7). What can you say about the red and blue segments? Do they overlap? Do they not overlap? Are they the same? Whatever happened, repeat this exercise until you have a drawing to illustrate each possibility:

- The red and blue segments overlap
- The red and blue segments do not overlap
- The red and blue segments are the same

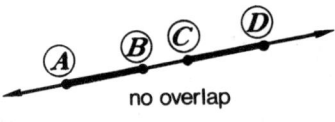

no overlap

Fig. 7

Exercise 3. Make a summary drawing of your results from exercises 1 and 2. First, organize the drawings from exercise 1. Then make many different choices for the red segment and blue segment. Make the drawings for each pair of choices, then label each drawing: overlap, no overlap, the same. Make as many different drawings as you can.

Project 2

Start with a line. Pick *one* point on the line (not two, as before) and erase the part of the line on one side of the point (fig. 8).

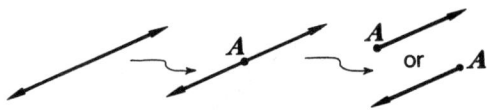

Fig. 8

This object is not a line segment (why?) and not a line (why?). It is a *ray*. Think of shining a flashlight from A, pointing in the direction of the arrow. The *endpoint* of the ray is A. Using A, we produced two rays from the line. If you think that A should be called a beginning point, you have a good sense of language. We could call A an apple or a horse or anything else, but we call A an endpoint because of its similarity to endpoints of line segments. Now let's look at the ways of making rays from lines and line segments.

Exercise 1. Make a drawing of a line similar to figure 9. Then make several copies, all on the same piece of tracing paper. On two copies, use a red pencil and draw the two rays that have A as an endpoint. On two other copies, use a blue pencil to draw the two rays that have B as an endpoint. Then you will have colored four drawings of rays.

Fig. 9

Make some more copies of figure 9. Pick one of the red rays and one of the blue rays. Copy them onto the same line. Do they overlap? Do they not overlap? Repeat using the same red ray, but with the other blue ray. Repeat again with other pairs of red and blue rays. Label each with the words *overlap* or *no overlap*.

Do not read on until you are finished with the preceding exercise. Have you made careful drawings? You should have found four different pairs: one red ray with one blue ray. If you found more or less, recheck your work. Three are labeled *overlap*. What can you say about the parts colored both red and blue? Are they lines? Line segments? Rays? Label them. (See fig. 10.)

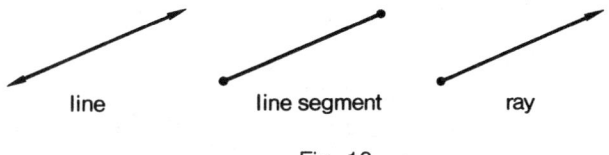

Fig. 10

- A *line* has no endpoints; it continues in two directions.
- A *line segment* has two endpoints.
- A *ray* has one endpoint and continues in one direction.

Exercise 2. Draw a line segment and label the endpoints X and Y. Copy it twice on tracing paper. On one copy, make a ray by extending an arrowhead at X. Extend the line segment on the other copy at Y. Each time the result is a ray. One has X as its endpoint; the other has Y.

Now draw three segments in a zigzag pattern similar to figure 11. Name the endpoints A, B, C, and D (fig. 11). Make several copies of your zigzag on the tracing paper.

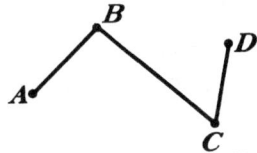

Fig. 11

On each copy, draw a ray in red with A, B, C, or D as its endpoint. Extend one of the line segments to produce the ray. (An example is shown in fig. 12.) Find as many rays as you can. How many of your rays begin with A? With B? With C? With D? (Remember what we said earlier about ending points and beginning points?)

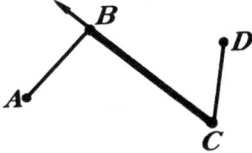

Fig. 12

Do not read on until you are finished with the preceding exercise. If you found one ray for A, two for B, two for C, and one for D, then you are on target. If not, recheck your work. Of course, many rays can have the same endpoint (look at fig. 13). But if we start with a line segment and use it as a guide, then we get only one ray for each endpoint.

Fig. 13

NCTM Projects to Enrich School Mathematics: Level 2

At last we can define an angle. You just drew several rays. Two of them had *B* as an endpoint; two of them had *C*. Let's draw them in pairs (fig. 14).

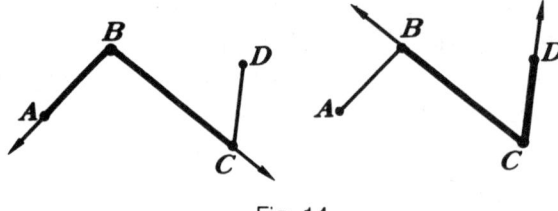

Fig. 14

In each drawing we see two rays sharing an endpoint. In each drawing we also see an angle. Whenever two line segments share an endpoint, we can construct two rays with that endpoint. Some examples are given in figure 15.

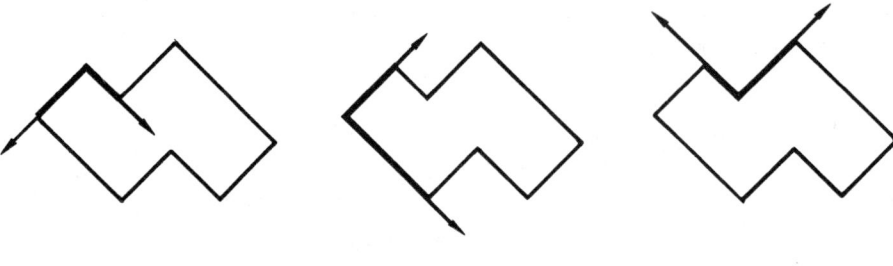

Fig. 15

An *angle* is two rays that share an endpoint. But the two rays must be *different* rays, and they must not be part of the same line (or else they would *be* that line). See figure 16.

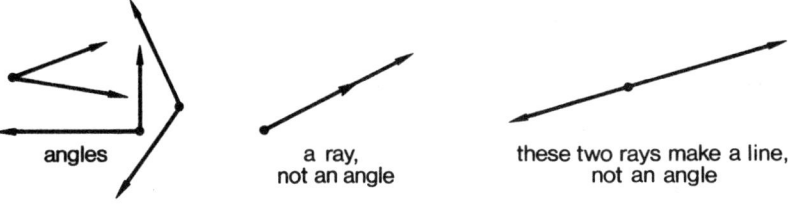

Fig. 16

One more term: The endpoint of an angle's two rays is called the *vertex* of that angle. Practice recognizing angles. How many can you trace in figure 13? (Remember that every pair of rays gives an angle.)

Project 3

Fold a piece of paper in half and then fold the crease back over itself as shown in figure 17. Use the corner where the two creases meet as a template (pattern) for drawing angles. Mark that corner with *T* on both sides of the template.

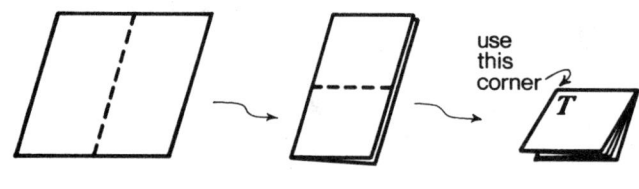

Fig. 17

On a clean sheet of paper, draw a point and call it *A*. Lay the template flat on the paper with its corner at

66   **NCTM Projects to Enrich School Mathematics: Level 2**

A. Draw line segments along the two sides of the template, inserting arrowheads for rays (fig. 18). Draw several more angles with the template to be sure of your technique.

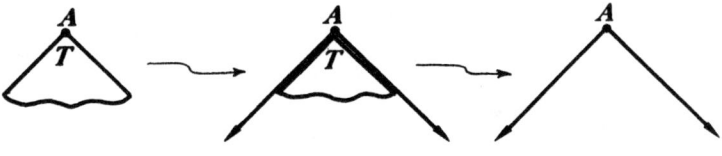

Fig. 18

Exercise 1. Take several pieces of paper, some of them oddly shaped. Make templates by folding each of them just as you did to make the first template. Draw a few angles with each template, all on the same page, then mix up the templates. Can you tell which template was used for which angles?

If you found that we can't tell the difference between templates by looking at the angles, then you are on target. If not, check your templates for careful folding and your drawing techniques for careful placement of the template.

The angle of the template is very special. In fact, angles equal to the angle of the template are so common that they have a collective name. They are all called *right angles.* You can use your template to draw right angles and to test angles to see if they are right angles or not.

Match the corner of the template to the vertex and lay one side of the template along one ray of the angle. Look at figure 19 for examples. Go back to your work in Project 2, exercise 2. Test all angles to find any right angles. Test the angles in figures 11 and 15. Some of those angles are right angles.

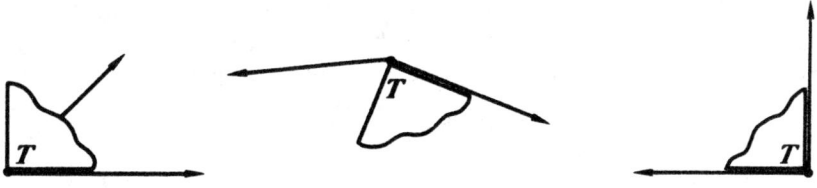

Fig. 19

Let's draw a zigzag using the template. Follow the pictures as they are numbered, using your template to draw on a clean sheet of paper (fig. 20).

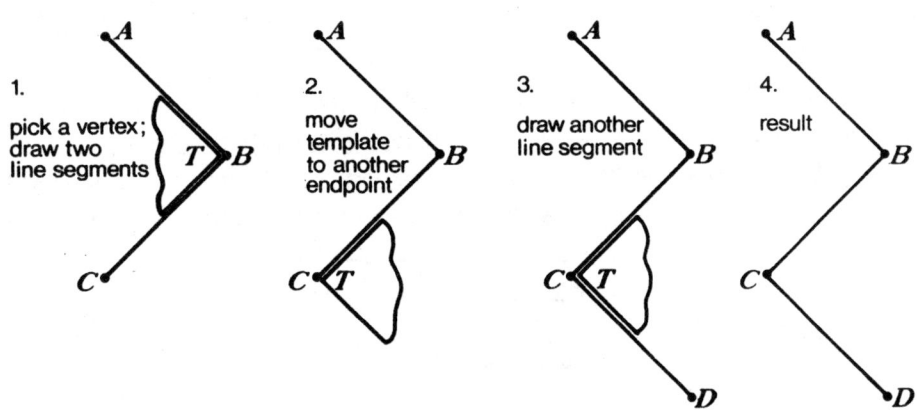

Fig. 20

Exercise 2. Make a long zigzag with your template. Now look back at the second step of figure 20. We had a choice; we could have put the template on the other side of the line segment connecting B and C, as in figure 21.

NCTM Projects to Enrich School Mathematics: Level 2

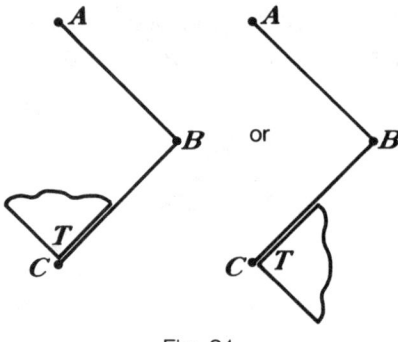

Fig. 21

Exercise 3. Make a drawing with your template similar to the spiral in figure 22.

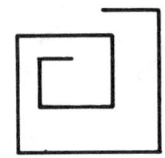

Fig. 22

Exercise 4. Draw a line segment from A to B. Begin a zigzag by drawing a right angle with vertex B. Continue to draw a chain of six line segments, using your template to draw each angle. End the sixth line segment at A.

Exercise 5. Do exercise 4 again, but this time draw a chain with four segments, ending the fourth line segment at A. Draw another with four segments, and then another. All these four-sided solutions should be familiar to you. They are rectangles; rectangles have four sides and every corner angle is a right angle. Now we have three four-sided shapes with all corner angles being right angles (fig. 23).

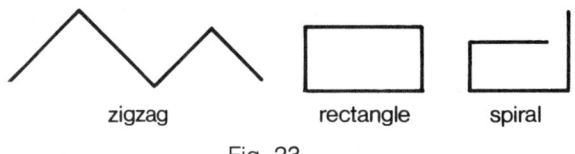

zigzag   rectangle   spiral

Fig. 23

What can we do with other numbers of sides? We can draw zigzags and spirals with any number of sides, so there isn't any challenge in them. One way to rule them both out is to require that shapes have no loose endpoints.

Rule 1: Every endpoint is the endpoint for exactly two line segments.

Exercise 6. For each number from 5 to 14, draw a shape with that number of sides so that in each shape all corner angles are right angles. Obey rule 1. Some spirals obey rule 1. But we can disregard them and make the problem more interesting by requiring that the line segments form a chain (fig. 24).

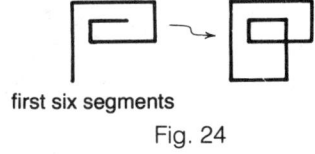

first six segments

Fig. 24

Rule 2: Line segments must not touch except at their endpoints.

Exercise 7. Repeat the preceding exercise, but obey rules 1 and 2. Did you draw an example for each number of sides? Could you draw an example with 48 sides? 54 sides? 11 037 sides?

Continue to build shapes with line segments while obeying rules 1 and 2. It is simpler in talking and writing to have a name for the shapes. A *polygon* is a collection of line segments drawn so that (1) every endpoint is the endpoint of exactly two line segments, and (2) no line segment touches another except at their endpoints.

Exercise 8. Study the examples in figure 25, then draw four different polygons with each number of sides from three to ten. Use your straightedge and imagination to make a neat, interesting display. What can you say about the number of sides and the number of angles for each polygon?

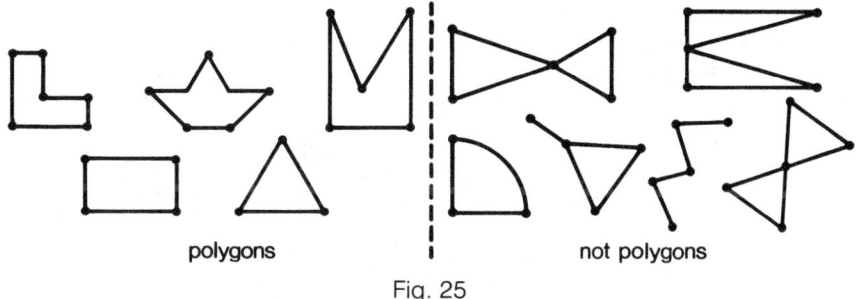

polygons | not polygons

Fig. 25

Project 4

By now you have drawn a large number of polygons. In doing Project 3, exercise 8, you drew several polygons for each number of sides (and you could surely have drawn even more). You had to be sure that every corner angle was a right angle. Notice, too, that each of the polygons for exercise 7 has an even number of sides—not 5, 13, or 11 037 sides, for instance. So an extra requirement can make a big difference in the results. Let's look at some other requirements.

First, we need two more ideas. In fact, you already met them when you tested the angles in figures 11 and 15 with the template to find the right angles. Please check them again. Then check the angles in figure 16. For each angle, one of three things can happen (fig. 26):

- The angle might be smaller than a right angle (the template angle).
- The angle might be larger than a right angle (the template angle).
- The angle might be a right angle.

acute angle   obtuse angle

Fig. 26

Of course, we have words to describe the angles:

- An *acute angle* is smaller than a right angle.
- An *obtuse angle* is larger than a right angle.

Test each angle of the polygon in figure 27 to find the acute angles. You should find three of them.

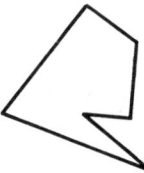

Fig. 27

Exercise 1. Review the polygons you drew for Project 3, exercise 8. Test each angle with your template. Label each acute angle with a special sign—you might use a "#," for instance. Some examples are shown in figure 28.

Fig. 28

Look at the chart in figure 29. This chart is for recording information about your polygons. We put a check in row five, column three, to show that there is a polygon with five angles that has exactly three acute angles in figure 28. There is also a polygon with four angles, none of which is acute, and a polygon with three angles, all of which are acute. An X means that no polygon is possible for that row and column. Of course, a polygon with three angles altogether cannot have four or five acute angles.

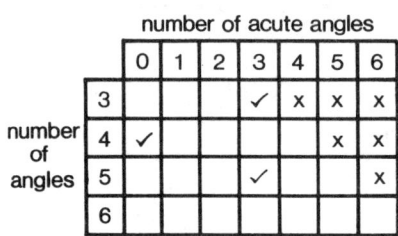

Fig. 29

Exercise 2. Make a chart similar to the one in figure 29. Look over your polygons from Project 3, exercise 8. Put appropriate checks on your chart based on the information in your drawings. Since you drew polygons with up to ten angles, you might want to make a chart to record all your information.

Exercise 3. Make a display for a bulletin board. Use several pieces of paper to make a chart similar to figure 29. The chart must be large enough to draw the polygons themselves in their places. Fill as many spots in your display as you can. This is a big job. You will want to look for ways to change a polygon in one spot to produce a polygon for a neighboring spot.

Project 5

If Project 4, exercise 3, wasn't enough of a challenge, we have one more restriction for you to try. Acuteness, obtuseness, and rightness are characteristic of angles but have nothing to do with where the angles come from. An angle can appear in wildly different polygons. Look at the variety of polygons you have drawn that have one or more right angles. Our next idea tells something about the way an angle relates to the polygon as a whole. Figure 30 shows several polygons with and without *indentations*. A polygon may have no indentations, one, or several indentations. An indentation may occur at an acute, a right, or an obtuse angle. A polygon with no indentations is called *convex*.

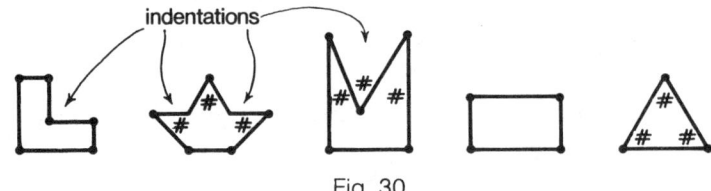

Fig. 30

Exercise 1. Review your drawings for Project 3, exercise 8. Check each polygon for indentations. Find all of the convex polygons. Make another chart. Use the chart to check off the *convex* polygons. In figure 30 there is a convex polygon with four angles, none acute, and a polygon with three angles, all acute. Put appropriate checks on your chart based on the information in your drawings for exercise 8. Again, you might want to make a chart to display all your information.

Exercise 2. Make another display of polygons as you did in Project 4, exercise 3. But in this display, draw only convex polygons. Be careful, you may find that some spots that had polygons before are empty now.

In comparing your polygon displays, you will see that there are many spots in the first display that cannot be filled in the second. A pattern should be clearly visible.

Exercise 3. Complete your project by making a glossary of the new words that you have learned. Include intelligible definitions and illustrations where appropriate.

Search into the origins of some of the words. Where does the word *angle* come from? *Right, acute,* and *obtuse* are terms that are used in other situations. How do their meanings change in different uses? Does their meaning in geometry help you to understand their other meanings? The word *polygon* has a prefix that occurs with many other words; what does *poly-* signify? A polygon with five angles is called a *pentagon*. Why? Find the standard names for polygons with from three to ten angles. What we have called an indentation is often called a *concavity* and is related to the term *concave*. Find out how *concave* is related to *convex,* and find some other uses for these words.

If you are interested in learning more about polygons or angles, look in your library for geometry books. A fascinating application of angles is in origami (or Japanese paper folding). Many beautiful and surprising shapes can be made by carefully folding a piece of paper.

Teacher Notes

Most treatments of angles introduce the idea of angle simultaneously with the idea of measurement of an angle with a protractor. With such an approach, students often identify an angle with its measure. Our early experience with line segments suggests learning about angles before learning about measuring angles. With a few simple tools, students of this unit can work with a variety of constructions designed to illuminate some basic properties of angles. The tone throughout is informal. The student will learn through experience in solving a series of construction problems.

Project 1 is devoted to laying a foundation of ideas and encouraging an attitude of care and precision in drawing. In exercise 1, there are six pairs of endpoints with which to define line segments: A with B, A with C, A with D, B with C, B with D, and C with D. In exercise 2, there are 6 × 6 = 36 pairs, red and blue. All choices for red and blue overlap, except two: red—A with B and blue—C with D; and red—C with D and blue—A with B. Of course in some cases, red and blue overlap in only a single point (such as red—A with B and blue—B with C). In other cases, red and blue are identical (such as red—A with B and blue—A with B).

Project 2 begins with a discussion of rays. There are two projects designed to clarify the distinctions among rays, lines, and line segments. With the basis secure, we introduce angles. Our definition may seem strange because it omits what are trivial angles and straight angles (that is, angles that measure 0 and 180 degrees, respectively). The purpose is to avoid the occasional special case in constructions and thus maintain a cleaner exposition. Our experience shows that students have no difficulty in expanding their idea of angles later.

Project 3 introduces a new tool—a right-angle template. The point of the first exercise is that all correctly constructed templates produce congruent angles. The notion of congruence is left implicit and informal. Note that all of the corner angles of the polygons in figure 15 are right angles.

After several relatively free constructions with the template, we begin to focus the work by introducing rules that will force construction of closed polygons. Following both rules in exercise 7, the student will find only polygons with an *even* number of sides and might, therefore, conjecture that no such construction can have an odd number of sides. This is a simple case of the important theorem (deferred for later studies) that the sum of the measures of the corner angles of a polygon with n angles equals the measure of $2n - 2$ right angles; that is, an even number of right angles. *Note:* A clever student might notice that disconnected collections of line segments might satisfy the definition of polygons. Two examples are drawn here:

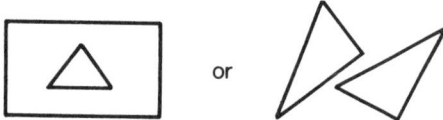

If this idea intrudes, praise the student for having noticed it, but suggest restricting all constructions to *simple polygons* (that is, polygons in which the collection of line segments defining the polygons are connected together).

Project 4 offers the opportunity to explore the effect of several restrictions on polygon constructions. The template is a convenient tool for defining acute and obtuse angles. Figure 27 has three acute angles, two right angles, and one obtuse angle. In exercise 2, the student will organize the polygon constructions according to numbers of acute angles. Of course, there is the obvious impossibility of a polygon's having more acute angles than it has angles altogether. Other than that restriction, all constructions are possible except that no triangle (three angles) can have exactly zero or one acute angle. Exercise 3 is a major task, if done well. There are techniques that aid in the constructions. For example:

shows a way to replace an obtuse angle with two obtuse angles. Using this technique, a polygon with seven angles, three of them acute, for example, can be altered into one with eight angles, three of them acute.

Project 5 is a reprise of Project 4 with the additional restriction of convexity. The maximum number of acute angles in this case is three.

This unit is related to a sequence of geometry lessons for the sixth-grade curriculum from the Comprehensive School Mathematics Program. In that context a somewhat different development leads to further study of polygons through a variety of constructions with a set of angle templates of several sizes. For further information consult *Geometry and Measurement, CSMP Mathematics for the Intermediate Grades,* Part VI, published by Mid-Continent Regional Educational Laboratory, Saint Louis, Missouri, 1980. Best wishes to you and your students. Comments on this unit will be welcomed by the author.

Explorations in Modular Arithmetic

J. PAUL McLAUGHLIN

ON WHAT day of the week were you born? Why will the day of the week be one day later this year than last year (in leap year, two days later)? On what day of the week will the first New Year's Day of the twenty-first century fall? If it is now 9 o'clock A.M., and a space ship is 135 hours into its flight and 77 hours from splashdown, what time did it blast off, and what time will it splash down?

These and many other questions can be answered using the techniques of modular arithmetic. In addition, there are many other applications, creative art forms, and discoveries that you can make using some of the things you learn in the exploration of modular arithmetic.

Keep a folder of your work as you complete this project. Some of the specific activities listed in the projects are described more fully in the Guide section. As you do these activities, look for patterns, think about other places where modular arithmetic or its principles can be used, develop your own methods for getting results, and think about how your methods could be used in related problems. Above all, use your ingenuity and be creative.

Projects

Project 1

1. Make a clockface with one movable hand (see fig. 1). For variety you may wish to use roman numerals instead of arabic numerals on your clock.

2. Make and complete an addition table using the clock as an aid.

Fig. 1. Clockface with movable hand

3. Make a subtraction table for the clock numbers, or else explain how to use the addition table to find answers for subtraction problems.

4. Complete activities A, B, and C in the Guide.

5. Prepare a report including the following tasks:

   a) Describe at least five patterns you find in the addition table.
   b) Describe the work you did in completing activities A, B, and C in the Guide.
   c) Develop a flowchart or an example detailing the steps you used in finding what time it will be a given number of hours from now and whether it will be A.M. or P.M.
   d) Write five problems in clock arithmetic.

Guide: The clock numbers are the counting numbers 1–12. Make a clockface with a movable hand. This will be used in solving certain problems involving time. For instance:

   It is now 9:00. If you are working on a project that will take six hours to complete, what time can you expect to finish?

To find the *clock sum* of two clock numbers, say 7 and 9, follow these steps:
- Set the hand at 12.
- Move the hand 7 hours forward (that is, clockwise).
- From that position move the hand another 9 hours forward.
- The numeral to which the hand now points is the clock sum of 7 and 9 (written 7 + 9).
- Record this result in the space where row 7 and column 9 intersect on the addition table (fig. 2).

+	1	2	3	4	5	6	7	8	9	10	11	12
1												
2								10			1	
3					8				12			
4							11				3	
5									2			
6										4		
7						1						
8								4				
9										7		9
10						5						10
11					4							11
12	1	2	3									12

Fig. 2. Addition table for clock numbers

You should verify the entries already given in the table to make sure you can use the rule, then complete the rest of the table. It may be helpful to use colored markers to highlight some of the patterns you discover in the table.

If you are not sure about the meaning of *commutative, associative,* and *identity number,* refer to Francis Mueller's article (Reference 4) or Karl J. Smith's book (Reference 5).

Activity A. Illustrate the *commutative property* for the addition of clock numbers ($a + b = b + a$, where a and b represent clock numbers).

Activity B. Describe how to find the sum of 5, 9, and 6 using (1) the clock and (2) the addition table.

Activity C. Give five examples illustrating the *associative property* for the addition of clock numbers: $a + (b + c) = (a + b) + c$, where a, b, and c represent clock numbers (but not necessarily *different* numbers).

Project 2

1. Complete an addition table and multiplication table for the calendar numbers (figs. 3 and 4).
2. Look for four patterns in the multiplication table and describe them.
3. Explain what is special or different about the numbers 0 and 1 in multiplication.
4. Show or describe how to use the multplication table to find the product of 3, 5, and 4.
5. Give work and additional examples called for in activities D, E, and F of the Guide.

Guide: Calendar arithmetic is based on the number of days in a week. Since the days of the week are not strictly numbered, we can let any day be the starting day in our system.

+	0	1	2	3	4	5	6
0	0						
1					4		
2						0	
3			5				
4							3
5				2			
6							5

Fig. 3. Addition table for calendar numbers

×	0	1	2	3	4	5	6
0		0		0			
1			2				
2					1		
3							4
4	0				5		
5							4
6			5				

Fig. 4. Multiplication table for calendar numbers

As an aid in completing the addition and multiplication tables, prepare a set of cards numbered 0, 1, 2, 3, 4, 5, and 6. Ordinary playing cards could be used—ace, 2, 3, 4, 5, 6, and 7—letting the ace represent 1 and relabeling 7 as 0. Keep the cards ordered at all times—do not shuffle them.

To find the sum of any numbers follow the steps below (here we are finding 4 + 5):

- Start with the deck of seven cards ordered with cards face up, 0 on top.
- Move a set of four cards from the top of the deck to the bottom.
- Now move a set of five cards from the top to the bottom of the deck.

The number of the card that is now on top is the *calendar sum* of 4 and 5. Use this procedure to check the entries already given in the addition table for calendar numbers and complete the table (fig. 3). *Question for thought:* If you move four cards one at a time, then five cards one at a time, would you get the sum of 4 and 5?

To find the product of two numbers, for example 3 × 4, start with the cards ordered, face up, 0 on top; move a set of four cards from the top to the bottom of the deck; move a second set of four cards, and a third set of four cards from the top to the bottom of the deck. You have now moved three sets of four cards each from the top to the bottom. The number of the top card is the product of 3 and 4. To ensure that you have mastered the technique, verify the results given in the multiplication table and complete the table (fig. 4). Use the results in the tables to complete activities D, E, and F. Use one of the references if you wish.

Activity D. Use the table in figure 4 to show that (3 × 5) × 4 = 3 × (5 × 4). Give four examples illustrating the associative property of multiplication of calendar numbers: (a × b) × c = a × (b × c) where a, b, and c represent calendar numbers (not necessarily different).

Activity E. Using the tables you completed for calendar arithmetic show that 3 × (4 + 2) = (3 × 4) + (3 × 2). Give four more examples illustrating that the multiplication of calendar numbers is distributive over the addition of calendar numbers.

Activity F. List all pairs of calendar numbers whose product is 1. Note that zero is not in any of these pairs.

Project 3

1. Write a definition of the terms *modulus, modulo, congruence* (of numbers), *congruence class, residue class,* and *multiplicative inverse.*

2. List several members in each of the residue classes modulo 7.

3. Make a multiplication table for modulo 5, modulo 6, and modulo 8.

4. For each of modulos 5, 6, 7, and 8, state which numbers do and which numbers do not have a multiplicative inverse.

Guide: References 1 and 5 will be useful for completing the activities in this project. Clock arithmetic is arithmetic modulo 12; calendar arithmetic is modulo 7. You could use the clock or the playing cards to complete the multiplication tables (fig. 5). Possibly a quicker way is to use the congruence class of the ordinary product. For example, in modulo 6 we use the numerals 0, 1, 2, 3, 4, and 5. In ordinary whole-number arithmetic, $3 \times 4 = 12$; 12 is congruent to 0 modulo 6; therefore $3 \times 4 = 0$ modulo 6.

Some of the entries for each of the multiplication tables are given for you. As usual, look for patterns in the tables as a help in completing the parts of this project.

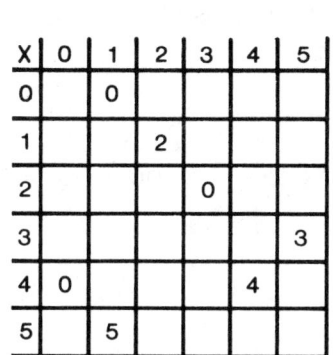

Multiplication table, modulo 6

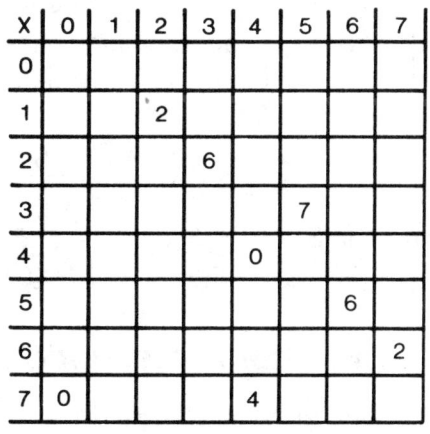

Multiplication table, modulo 8

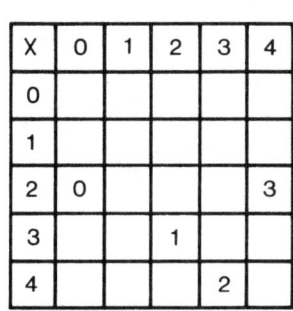

Multiplication table, modulo 5

Fig. 5. Modulo multiplication tables

Project 4

1. Calculate the day of the week on which you were born.

2. Calculate the day of the week on which the Declaration of Independence was signed (4 July 1776), and check your answer in a history book.

3. Select ten dates, past or future (some less than a year away), and determine the day of the week for each of the dates.

4. Write a brief description of your rule for finding the day of the week for a given day, month, and year.

Guide: Follow the procedure outlined below for finding the day of the week for any past or future date. To begin, you need a known reference date. For example, to find the day of the week on which you were born you need to know the day of the week for your last, or next, birthday and your exact age in days on that birthday. In finding your exact age in days don't forget to add in one extra day for each leap year (29 February) you have lived. Divide your age in days by 7 and note the remainder. Count backward from the day of the week for this year's birthday as many days as the remainder. If you have made no mistakes, this is the day of the week on which you were born. Example: Suppose you were fourteen years old on your last birthday, which was Sunday, 4 July 1982. This means you were born in 1968. You check and discover that you have seen three leap years—three February 29s. Thus your age in days is $(14 \times 365) + 3$, or 5110 days; 5110 divided by 7 is 730, remainder 3. Count three days backward from Sunday (the day of your last birthday)—Saturday, Friday, Thursday. You were born on Thursday—Thursday, 4 July 1968.

In working problems of this type, count backward if you want the day of the week for a past date and forward for a future date. Don't forget leap years. Leap years are divisible by 4, with those ending in 00 divisible by 400. Note that 1900 and 1800 were *not* leap years; 2000 will be a leap year; 2100, 2200, and 2300 will not be leap years. You cannot go back past the mid-1700s when the present calendar was instituted without making further corrections.

Another rule makes use of the fact that the day of the week for a given calendar date advances one day each year except leap year, when it advances two days.

NCTM Projects to Enrich School Mathematics: Level 2

Project 5

1. Prepare the six drawings for modular art modulo 7, discussed in the Guide.
2. Write a brief explanation of why two rows may produce the same picture.
3. Prepare at least three other modular art pictures or drawings using the references for ideas and suggestions.

Guide: Use Reference 1 and Reference 5 (pages 221–23) for completing this project. For the first part you need the multiplication table for calendar arithmetic (fig. 4). Ignore the 0 row and 0 column. You will also need a compass, ruler, protractor, and colored markers or crayons. For each of the drawings for modulo 7, draw a circle and mark six equally spaced points on the circle (use central angles of 360°/6, or 60°, to locate the points). Number the points 1 through 6. Write down one of the rows of the table—row 3, for example:

x	1	2	3	4	5	6
3	3	6	2	5	1	4

On the circle draw segments joining 1 to 3, 2 to 6, 3 to 2, 4 to 5, 5 to 1, and 6 to 4. This drawing would be labeled (7, 3) for modulo 7 row 3. Color your picture according to your taste.

Further Investigations

Construct a division table for calendar numbers using a deck of cards. As an example, to find 4 ÷ 3, start with 4 on top; move a set of three cards from the bottom to the top and check the top card. If the top card is 0, then 4 divided by 3 is 1. If it is not 0 repeat with another set of three moved from the bottom to the top. Continue the process, counting the number of sets of three that are moved from the bottom to the top until 0 is the top card. The number of sets of three you must transfer from bottom to top is the *calendar quotient* of 4 divided by 3.

Other forms of modular art and curve stitching on the circle are interesting topics for further investigation.

REFERENCES

1. Forseth, Sonia, and Andria Price Troutman. "Using Mathematical Structures to Generate Artistic Designs." *Mathematics Teacher* 67 (May 1974): 393–98.
2. Law, Carol. "Arithmetical Congruences with Practical Applications." *Mathematics Magazine* 31 (March–April 1948): 221–27.
3. Meserve, Bruce E., and Max A. Sobel. *Contemporary Mathematics,* pp. 94–100. 3d ed. Englewood Cliffs, N.J.: Prentice-Hall, 1981.
4. Mueller, Francis J. "Modular Arithmetic." In *Enrichment Mathematics for the Grades,* Twenty-seventh Yearbook of the National Council of Teachers of Mathematics, edited by Julius H. Hlavaty, pp. 73–91. Washington, D.C.: The Council, 1963.
5. Smith, Karl J. *The Nature of Modern Mathematics,* pp. 204–10, 221–25. 2d ed. Monterey, Calif.: Brooks/Cole Publishing Co., 1976.
6. Stewart, B. M. *Theory of Numbers.* 2d ed. New York: Macmillan Publishing Co., 1965.

Teacher Notes

Several discovery or creative types of activities are used in this unit. The opportunity for students to display their work should encourage other students to try similar projects. Some of the work is appropriate for bulletin board display, and some, such as the student's folder, could be displayed on an interest table.

Many of the activities are self-checking in that the student describes patterns, explains a rule or method, or verifies results through some independent source. The Twenty-seventh Yearbook of the National Council of Teachers of Mathematics (Reference 4) is particularly helpful in completing the tables. Karl Smith's book (Reference 5) has several illustrations of modular art and suggestions for other activities. A copy of this book should be available for the student.

The tables for the projects are shown in figures 1–6. Some of the patterns students describe might be as follows:

Table for Project 1

+	1	2	3	4	5	6	7	8	9	10	11	12
1	2	3	4	5	6	7	8	9	10	11	12	1
2	3	4	5	6	7	8	9	10	11	12	1	2
3	4	5	6	7	8	9	10	11	12	1	2	3
4	5	6	7	8	9	10	11	12	1	2	3	4
5	6	7	8	9	10	11	12	1	2	3	4	5
6	7	8	9	10	11	12	1	2	3	4	5	6
7	8	9	10	11	12	1	2	3	4	5	6	7
8	9	10	11	12	1	2	3	4	5	6	7	8
9	10	11	12	1	2	3	4	5	6	7	8	9
10	11	12	1	2	3	4	5	6	7	8	9	10
11	12	1	2	3	4	5	6	7	8	9	10	11
12	1	2	3	4	5	6	7	8	9	10	11	12

Fig. 1. Addition table, clock numbers

Tables for Project 2

+	0	1	2	3	4	5	6
0	0	1	2	3	4	5	6
1	1	2	3	4	5	6	0
2	2	3	4	5	6	0	1
3	3	4	5	6	0	1	2
4	4	5	6	0	1	2	3
5	5	6	0	1	2	3	4
6	6	0	1	2	3	4	5

Fig. 2. Addition table for calendar numbers

×	0	1	2	3	4	5	6
0	0	0	0	0	0	0	0
1	0	1	2	3	4	5	6
2	0	2	4	6	1	3	5
3	0	3	6	2	5	1	4
4	0	4	1	5	2	6	3
5	0	5	3	1	6	4	2
6	0	6	5	4	3	2	1

Fig. 3. Multiplication table for calendar numbers

Tables for Project 3

×	0	1	2	3	4
0	0	0	0	0	0
1	0	1	2	3	4
2	0	2	4	1	3
3	0	3	1	4	2
4	0	4	3	2	1

Fig. 4. Multiplication table, modulo 5

×	0	1	2	3	4	5
0	0	0	0	0	0	0
1	0	1	2	3	4	5
2	0	2	4	0	2	4
3	0	3	0	3	0	3
4	0	4	2	0	4	2
5	0	5	4	3	2	1

Fig. 5. Multiplication table, modulo 6

×	0	1	2	3	4	5	6	7
0	0	0	0	0	0	0	0	0
1	0	1	2	3	4	5	6	7
2	0	2	4	6	0	2	4	6
3	0	3	6	1	4	7	2	5
4	0	4	0	4	0	4	0	4
5	0	5	3	7	4	1	6	3
6	0	6	4	2	0	6	4	2
7	0	7	6	5	4	3	2	1

Fig. 6. Multiplication table, modulo 8

- For each row there is a corresponding column.
- In addition tables the numbers increase by 1 as you go across the table.
- Diagonals (lower left to upper right) all have the same numbers for the addition tables.
- Each number appears exactly once in each row and each column of the addition tables and in the multiplication tables for 5 and 7 (this is not true for multiplication tables for 6 and 8).
- In clock arithmetic 12 plus any number is that number. Twelve is the identity number for addition in clock numbers.

Project 1

Activity B. To find the clock sum of three numbers on the clock (e.g., 5 + 9 + 6): Start at 12, move 5 hours forward, then 9 hours forward, and finally 6 more hours forward. The numeral to which the hand now points is the answer to the clock sum of 5, 9, and 6. To find the sum of 5, 9, and 6 using the table: (5 + 9) + 6, find the sum of 5 and 9 in the table—5 + 9 = 2. Now find the sum of 2 and 6 in the table—2 + 6 = 8.

Activity C. (5 + 9) + 6 = 5 + (9 + 6) is an example of the associative property of the addition of calendar numbers.

To find the time 19 hours from now, use the division property of whole numbers to write 19 as (1 × 12) + 7. Likewise, 29 = (2 × 12) + 5, and 79 = (6 × 12) + 7.

If it is now 9 A.M., then in 19 hours it will be 9 + 19 = 9 + (12 + 7) = 9 + 7 = 4. To determine if it will be A.M. or P.M., count the number of times 12 is "added"; for an even number of twelves the A.M./P.M. designation stays the same, but for an odd number of twelves the designation changes. Note that 7 + 9 comes after 12 in the addition table; so in finding 9 + 19, 12 is added twice and the designation stays the same: 19 hours after 9 A.M. is 4 A.M. Here is an alternative method of finding the time and the A.M./P.M. designation. To find the time nineteen hours after 9 A.M., add 9 and 19: 9 + 19 = 28. Now divide the sum by 24 and look at the remainder (in this case 4). If the remainder is less than 12, the remainder is the time and the A.M./P.M. designation is the same as at the start (in this case, A.M.). If the remainder is more than 12, subtract 12 from the remainder. The difference is the time and the A.M./P.M. designation is the opposite of the original.

Project 2

3. The product of 0 and any number is 0. The product of 1 and any number is that number; 1 is the identity for multiplication or multiplicative identity.

4 and **Activity D.** To find the product of 3, 5, and 4 in calendar arithmetic use either (3 × 5) × 4 or 3 × (5 × 4). For (3 × 5) × 4, find the product of 3 and 5 in row 3, column 5: 3 × 5 = 1. Now find the product of 1 and 4 in row 1, column 4: 1 × 4 = 4. Thus (3 × 5) × 4 = 4. To find the product of 3 × (5 × 4), find the product of 5 and 4 in row 5, column 4: 5 × 4 = 6. Now find 3 × 6 in row 3, column 6: 3 × 6 = 4. Therefore 3 × (5 × 4) = 4. Note that (3 × 5) × 4 = 3 × (5 × 4), an example of the associative property of the multiplication of calendar numbers.

Activity E. To illustrate the distributive property of multiplication over addition—3 × (4 + 2)—find 4 + 2 = 6 in the addition table and then 3 × 6 = 4 in the multiplication table. For the left member—(3 × 4) + (3 × 2)—find 3 × 4 = 5 and 3 × 2 = 6 in the multiplication table, then find 5 + 6 = 4 in the addition table.

Activity F. The following pairs have a product of 1: 1 and 1, 2 and 4, 3 and 5, 6 and 6. The product of 0 and any number is 0.

Project 3

Residue classes. When a number n is divided by 7, the remainder is the residue class to which the number belongs. Thus,

Class 0 includes 0, 7, 14, 21, and so on.
Class 1: 1, 8, 15, 22, 29, . . .
Class 2: 2, 9, 16, 23, 30, . . .
Class 3: 3, 10, 17, 24, 31, . . .
Class 4: 4, 11, 18, 25, 32, 39, . . .
Class 5: 5, 12, 19, 26, 33, 40, 47, . . .
Class 6: 6, 13, 20, 27, 34, 41, 48, . . .

Residue classes for any other moduli are defined in a similar way.

For multiplicative inverses, note that zero does not have a multiplicative inverse in any modulo system. Each number except 0 has a multiplicative inverse in mod 5 and in mod 7.

In mod 6 the numbers 1 and 5 have multiplicative inverses. The numbers 2, 3, and 4 do not have multiplicative inverses. Note that 1 and 5 are relatively prime to 6, whereas 2, 3, and 4 are not relatively prime to 6.

In modulo 8, the numbers 1, 3, 5, and 7 have multiplicative inverses and are relatively prime to 8, whereas the numbers 2, 4, and 6 do not have multiplicative inverses and are not relatively prime to 8.

Project 4

The Declaration of Independence was approved on Thursday, 4 July 1776. To calculate this there are 75 239 days from 4 July 1776 to Sunday, 4 July 1982 (206 years, of which 49 were leap years, thus (206 × 365) + 49. (1800 and 1900 were *not* leap years.) 75 239 divided by 7 is 10 748 remainder 3. An alternative method: 206 days for 206 years plus 49 days for the 49 February 29s = 206 + 49 = 255 = (36 × 7) + 3. Counting three days back from Sunday gives Thursday.

Project 5

The six patterns for modular 7 are shown in figure 7. The pattern for (7, 1) is just the pattern joining one to each number. The other five are more interesting. For any modulus n the pattern for $(n, 1)$ and $(n, n - 1)$ will always be like (7, 1) and (7, 6). To see why two patterns are the same, note that those pairs of numbers whose product is 1 (modulo 7) will result in essentially the same picture. That is, two numbers that are multiplicative inverses in the given modulus will result in the same picture. Smith's book (Reference 5) is a good reference here. There are numerous other ways in which the addition or multiplication table for some finite system is used to create patterns and designs.

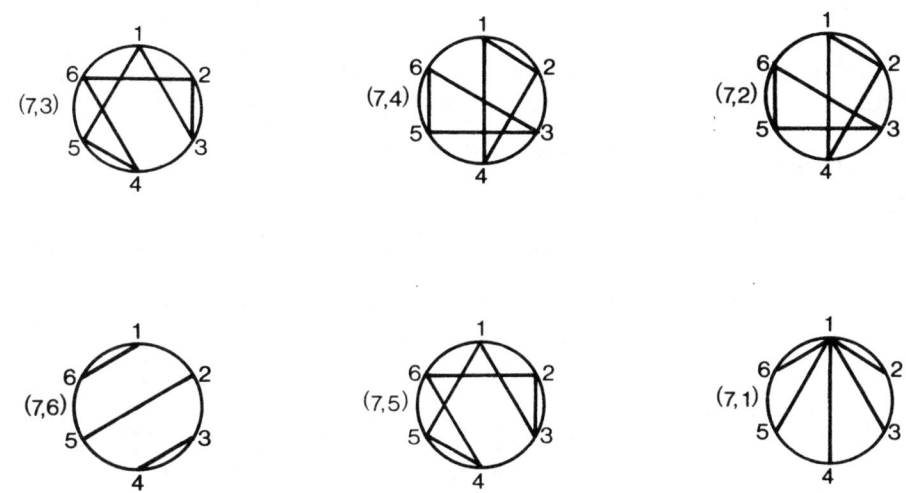

Fig. 7. Patterns for modular art (modulo 7)

Investigating Programming Languages

BETTY TRAVIS

DURING the past thirty years, more than two hundred programming languages have been developed, each within a unique environment and each to fulfill a particular need. The knowledge and study of a variety of languages can improve your vocabulary of computer programming terms and help you to understand better the languages you already know and make better decisions in choosing a language for future use.

Projects

Project 1

Write a brief history of five programming languages, naming persons or environments responsible for the development of the particular language. The purpose of the language should also be stated.

Guide: Possible languages could include APL, COBOL, FORTRAN, LISP, Pascal, PILOT, PL/1, or SNOBOL. References 1 and 3 are helpful.

For example, BASIC (Beginner's All-purpose Symbolic Instruction Code) was originally developed in 1964–1965 at Dartmouth College by Thomas Kurtz and John Kemeny as an interactive language to be used in an educational environment. Today, BASIC is one of the most widely used languages with microcomputer and small business-oriented computer systems.

Project 2

Determine the most widely used programming languages in your community by surveying ten businesses. If there is a college or university in your area, contact the computer science department or the business data systems department to determine the programming languages being taught at that institution. Write a brief description of your results.

Project 3

Write a definition of *structured programming*.

Guide: References 2, 5, and 6 can give you information on structured programming. You should be able to discuss the advantages of using structured programming.

Project 4

Using the languages you selected for Project 1, write definitions of at least ten instruction statements in each language and give an example of each instruction as it would be used in a program. References 1 and 3 will be especially helpful.

Guide: For example, several instruction statements in BASIC would be these:

REM: the statement used to insert remarks into the program for other users and future reference. It is not executable.
```
10 REM This REM statement is for remarks.
```

PRINT: the statement used to print statements and answers and to give output during a run of the program.
```
10 PRINT 3 * 4
```

LET: the "assignment" statement that allows the programmer to assign a value to a variable.
```
10 LET A = 3
20 LET A = A + 1
```

FOR/NEXT: program control statements that set up a repeating loop to direct the flow of operations within a program.
```
10 FOR C = 1 TO 10
50 NEXT C
```

Project 5

Select two of the five languages you have investigated and write a short program to print the integers 1 to 100.

Guide: For example, the program in BASIC would be this:
```
10 For I = 1 TO 100
20 PRINT I
30 NEXT I
40 END
```

Further Investigations

If you are interested in programming languages, you might want to write the program in Project 5 in several other languages, varying the format of output.

To continue in this study, you might want to investigate the differences between machine-level and assembler languages and the high-level programming languages you have discussed.

REFERENCES

1. ACM SIGPLAN (Association of Computing Machinery Special Interest Group on Programming Languages). *History of Programming Languages.* Vol. 13, no. 8. Proceedings of the History of Programming Languages Conference, Los Angeles, 1–3 June 1978, edited by Richard L. Wexelblat. New York: Association for Computing Machinery, 1978.
2. Andree, Richard V., Josephine P. Andree, and David D. Andree. *Computer Programming: Techniques, Analysis and Mathematics.* Englewood Cliffs, N.J.: Prentice-Hall, 1973.
3. Helms, Harry. *Computer Languages Reference Guide.* Indianapolis: Howard W. Sams & Co., 1981.
4. Maisel, Herbert. *Computers: Programming and Applications.* Chicago: Science Research Associates, 1976.
5. Organick, Elliott I., Alexandra I. Forsythe, and Robert P. Plummer. *Programming Language Structure.* New York: Academic Press, 1978.
6. Pratt, Terrence W. *Programming Language: Design and Implementation.* Englewood Cliffs, N.J.: Prentice-Hall, 1975.
7. Pakin, Sandra. *APL: A Short Course.* Englewood Cliffs, N.J.: Prentice-Hall, 1973.

Teacher Notes

Project 1

APL (<u>A</u> <u>P</u>rogramming <u>L</u>anguage): APL was first defined by K. E. Iverson in <u>A</u> <u>P</u>rogramming <u>L</u>anguage (Wiley 1962) and has since been developed in collaboration with A. D. Falkoff. The language was developed as a tool in data processing and for use in teaching classes.

COBOL (<u>CO</u>mmon <u>B</u>usiness <u>O</u>riented <u>L</u>anguage): A committee of computer users and consultants, manufacturers, and government employees was responsible for its development in late 1959 and early 1960. The language was to be a problem-oriented but machine-independent common language for business problems.

FORTRAN (<u>FOR</u>mula <u>TRAN</u>slation): FORTRAN was developed by IBM in 1957 and was designed as an applied programming language to be used by mathematicians, scientists, and engineers. The most significant advantage of FORTRAN is the ease in which complex mathematical expressions and operations can be handled through the use of arithmetic operations.

Pascal: The language Pascal, named after the French mathematician Blaise Pascal (1623–1662), was developed by Niklaus Wirth, a computer scientist at the Institut für Informatik in Zurich, Switzerland, during the late 1960s. It was one of the first major programming languages developed after the concept of structured programming.

PL/1 (<u>P</u>rogramming <u>L</u>anguage 1): PL/1 was developed by IBM in the early 1960s to respond to the need for a more common programming language between scientific and business users. The designers used the arithmetic and computational abilities of FORTRAN and the data-processing characteristics of COBOL.

LISP (<u>LIS</u>t <u>P</u>rocessing): LISP was developed in the late 1950s and early 1960s by John McCarthy and Marvin Minsky of MIT as a language used in artificial intelligence studies. LISP is characterized by computing with symbolic expressions rather than numbers and by representing information in the memory of a computer by list structure.

SNOBOL (<u>S</u>tri<u>N</u>g <u>O</u>riented Sym<u>BO</u>lic <u>L</u>anguage): SNOBOL was developed in 1962 by Ralph Griswold, Ivan Polonsky, and Dave Farber at the Programming Research Studies Department at Bell Telephone Laboratories. The main characteristic of the language is the ease of character string manipulation and processing.

Project 3

Structured programming is a method of programming in which three basic control structures are used to develop programs. Structured programming was developed as the computer and data-processing industry matured in the 1960s. It was evident that there was a need for a structure and design to programs so that the programs would be reliable and easy to modify and maintain. Two mathematicians, Corrado Bohm and Giuseppe Jacopini, are credited with the beginning of structured programming theory. At the 1964 International Colloquium on Algebraic Linguistics and Automata Theory in Israel, Bohm and Jacopini proposed three basic control structures to express all programming logic. These control structures are (1) sequence, (2) if-then-else, and (3) do-while. The sequence control structure implies one event occurs immediately after another. The if-then-else structure is used for conditional statements and decisions. Program looping is allowed with the use of the do-while control structure.

Project 4 (See References.)

Project 5

There are different ways to write a program in the same language. The following programs could be used as models.

APL

```
        I ← 0
NEXT:   → (100 < I ← I + 1)/0
        I
        → NEXT
```

Pascal
```
PROGRAM NUMBER (INPUT, OUTPUT);
VAR N: INTEGER;
BEGIN
     FOR N: = 1 TO 100 DO WRITELN(N);
END.
```
FORTRAN IV
```
     DO 25 N = 1, 100
       WRITE (6, 100)N
  25 CONTINUE
 100 FORMAT (I3)
     STOP
     END
```
PL/1
```
NUMBER:  PROCEDURE OPTIONS (MAIN);
         DECLARE (X) FIXED BIN;
         DO X = 1 TO 100;
              PUT SKIP LIST (X);
         END;
         END NUMBER;
```

Since there are several correct versions of programming in a single language, it is difficult to write a "solution" to this project. It is recommended that the teacher who doesn't feel qualified to check these make arrangements with the computer science department at a local college or university to have the students' programs checked.

Archimedes

ROBERT BUSS

ARCHIMEDES is considered one of the three greatest mathematicians ever to have lived. The other two were Newton and Gauss. For a proper understanding of Archimedes' work, we need to be somewhat familiar with his life and times. The reference list will help you, and your school or community library probably contains additional sources you will wish to explore. Archimedes was a famous man and much has been written about him.

Projects

Project 1

Write a short paragraph answering each of the following questions.

1. When and where did Archimedes live and die? What was his father's name and occupation? (See Reference 1.)

2. Other well-known Greek mathematicians were Pythagoras and Euclid. When did Archimedes live in relation to these two mathematicians? (See Reference 1.)

Project 2

There are a number of stories commonly told about Archimedes. Your task is to find these stories and to rewrite them in your own words.

1. Archimedes and the golden crown. (See Reference 2.)

2. Archimedes burning the ships of the Roman fleet with his mirrors. It so happens that a scientist in the 1970s tried to duplicate Archimedes' achievement—you will want to report on these results. (See References 3 and 4.)

3. The death of Archimedes. (See Reference 9.)

Project 3

1. About eleven works of Archimedes still exist. To get an appreciation of the types of problems that he worked on, list the titles of his works. (See Reference 6.)

2. One of his books is called *The Sandreckoner*. What is the problem that Archimedes solved in this book? (See Reference 6.)

Project 4

Tell the story of how Archimedes' method was rediscovered. As you do, tell who J. L. Heiberg was and where the lost work was rediscovered. Tell how the work had nearly been erased. Tell what other works of Archimedes' were found at the same time. (See References 7 and 8.)

Guide: It was known that Archimedes wrote a description of how he had made his mathematical discoveries before he proceeded to a formal proof. For centuries no one knew if a copy still existed, and it was feared to have been lost forever. The discovery of this lost work in the twentieth century is one of the more exciting stories to be told in the history of mathematics. This tale is not too well known, and you will have to work a bit to come up with the story. The references will probably be harder than most to find—you may have to search them out in a university or large public library—but the story is a good one and the effort will be worth it. (See References 7 and 8.)

Project 5

In the second proposition of his method, Archimedes "proved" that the volume of a sphere is four times that of a certain related cylinder. What cylinder? Explain Archimedes' construction. Notice how Archimedes uses mechanics to *do* algebra. Carefully follow each step and show how the conclusion follows.

Guide: This will be tougher going, but anything worthwhile takes some effort. Here we want to "go into Archimedes' workshop" and see how he got the original ideas for his later, more complete works. You will see how Archimedes used his knowledge of mechanical matters to compensate for his ignorance of algebra (it hadn't been invented yet). Rewrite Archimedes' proof and give a reason for each of his steps. Show exactly how Archimedes used a mechanical approach to reach his conclusion. (See Reference 7. If this is too difficult, see Reference 6 as described in Project 3.)

REFERENCES

1. Bell, Eric Temple. *Men of Mathematics.* New York: Simon & Schuster, 1962.
2. Vitruvius. "On Architecture." In *The World of Mathematics,* vol. 1, p. 185, edited by James R. Newman. New York: Simon & Schuster, 1956.
3. Tzetzes. "Book of Histories." In *The World of Mathematics,* vol. 1, p. 187, edited by James R. Newman. New York: Simon & Schuster, 1956.
4. "Archimedes' Weapon." *Time,* 26 November 1973.
5. Eves, Howard. *An Introduction to the History of Mathematics.* New York: Holt, Rinehart & Winston, 1976.
6. Hutchins, Robert M., and J. Mortimer Adler, eds. *Great Books of the Western World,* vol. 2. Chicago: University of Chicago Press, 1952.
7. Heath, Thomas L., ed. *The Works of Archimedes.* New York: Dover Publications, 1953.
8. Smith, David Eugene. "A Newly Discovered Treatise of Archimedes." *Monist* 19 (1909): 202–30.
9. Plutarch. "Marcellus." In *Lives of the Noble Romans,* pp. 101–6. New York: Dell Publishing Co., 1972.

Teacher Notes

These are the essential facts. Teachers may require more details.

Project 1

1. Archimedes was born about 287 B.C. and died in 212 B.C. at about the age of 75. He was born and died in the city of Syracuse in Sicily. His father's name was Pheidias and he was an astronomer.

2. Pythagoras—569?–500? B.C.
   Euclid—exact dates uncertain; probably was born about 365 B.C.
   Archimedes—287?–212 B.C.

Project 2

1. Archimedes was asked to determine whether a crown was solid gold. He solved the problem by immersing it in water. A solid that is heavier than a fluid will, when placed in that fluid, descend to the bottom; when the solid is weighed in the fluid, it is lighter than its true weight by the weight of the fluid displaced.

2. Archimedes is said to have focused the sun's rays to set fire to the attacking Roman fleet. In 1973, historian Ionnis Sakkas tried to duplicate this feat with 70 mirror-bearing sailors at the naval base outside Athens. A target began to smoke in three seconds and was soon engulfed in flames. Sakkas used flat mirrors covered with polished copper.

3. Archimedes died when the Romans captured Syracuse. One story has it that a Roman soldier killed Archimedes after telling him to stand away from some geometrical drawings that Archimedes had made on the ground.

Project 3

1. Archimedes' works include the following:
   - On the Sphere and the Cylinder
   - Measurement of a Circle
   - On Conoids and Spheroids
   - On Spirals
   - On the Equilibrium of Planes
   - The Sandreckoner
   - Quadrature of the Parabola
   - On Floating Bodies
   - Book of Lemmas
   - The Cattle Problem
   - The Method

2. The thesis of *The Sandreckoner* is that it is possible to write a number greater than the number of grains of sand in the universe. This problem is meaningful when we recall that the Greeks did not have our place-value notation for the numbers.

Project 4

A scholar noted some partially erased mathematical work on a parchment he discovered in a monastery in Constantinople. He published his finding. J. L. Heiberg, scholar of Greek mathematics, read this account and came to investigate the find. The common practice was to erase an older work for a new one and thus Archimedes' method was nearly lost in the tenth century. With the method were also found some of Archimedes' previously known works including *On Floating Bodies*, of which no known Greek text was then available.

Project 5

The cylinder in question has a base equal to a great circle of the given sphere and with the height equal to the sphere's diameter. Archimedes (lacking algebra) considered chords and segments as actual physical entities and moved them about a fulcrum—much as we move terms about the equal sign of an equation.

Ancient Numeration Systems

GEORGE H. WILLSON

MATHEMATICS uses many symbols to express ideas that are almost taken for granted when dealing with this discipline. In your mathematics training you have seen mathematical sentences, ratios, and numerals used to express certain ideas, for example, the use of a numeral to express or name a number. Therefore, the purpose of your work in numeration systems is to learn more about the naming of numbers in our decimal system. In addition, you will examine other numeration systems with an emphasis on those of their properties that can shed light on the properties of our familiar decimal system. Even though some of these systems are quite ancient, it is of interest to note the similarities between them and the system we use today.

Projects

Project 1

Study the **tally** numeration system. As you complete the tasks for this system and the tasks for Projects 2–5, fill in the chart below to record information about properties of the five numeration systems we are considering.

Properties	Numeration Systems				
	Tally	Egyptian	Roman	Babylonian	Mayan
Addition Repetition Base Place value					

1. Determine which of the properties in the left-hand column of the chart are used in the tally system. Mark an "X" on the chart for each one that is used.

2. Write a brief explanation of how the tally system works and give an example of its use in our modern society. (*Hint:* Keeping score for a game.)

Guide: Reference 5 will provide the information you need for the tally system. Books on the teaching of arithmetic as well as encyclopedias will provide general information on numeration systems.

Project 2

Write an explanation of the numeration system used by the Egyptians. Complete the following tasks for this system:

1. Determine what properties are used in the Egyptian system and enter them on your chart.

2. Learn to read and write the number symbols used by the Egyptians. For example, how would you write the numeral 432 in Egyptian numerals? (*Note:* There may be some differences in the symbols presented by different sources.)

NCTM Projects to Enrich School Mathematics: Level 2

3. Write a brief explanation of how the system works. (*Note:* Include the base they used and note how this compares with our decimal system.)

Guide: References 1, 2, 3, 4, and 5 will give you information on the Egyptian system. In addition, other encyclopedias and many books on the teaching of arithmetic contain sections or chapters on numeration systems.

Project 3

Write an explanation of the numeration system used by the Romans. For this system, complete the following tasks:

1. Learn to read and write the symbols used by the Romans. Write the present year using Roman numerals. (*Note:* What does it mean when a smaller numeral is written before a larger numeral?)

2. Identify the properties associated with the Roman system and enter the data on your chart. Note the similarities and the differences among the tally, Egyptian, and Roman systems.

3. What special symbols other than X, C, and M did the Romans use to indicate how they grouped? (*Hint:* Look at the symbols V, L, and D.)

4. Write a brief explanation of how the Roman system works and give examples of its use in our modern society.

Guide: To obtain the necessary information, use References 1, 2, 3, 4, and 5. Again, encyclopedias and many books on the teaching of arithmetic will contain sections or chapters on numeration systems.

Project 4

Write an explanation of the numeration system used by the Babylonians. Complete the following tasks for this system:

1. Learn to read and write the symbols used by the Babylonians. How do you think they wrote the numeral 1? 60? 3600? How did they handle the numerals 1–59?

2. Identify the properties of the Babylonian system and enter them on your chart.

3. Compare the similarities and differences of the Babylonian, Egyptian, and Roman systems. Concentrate on the properties of each one.

4. Write a brief explanation of how the Babylonian system works and include some vestiges that remain today.

Guide: Use References 1, 2, 3, 4, and 5 to obtain the necessary information. The use of encyclopedias as well as many books on the teaching of arithmetic will provide the needed information for this system.

Project 5

Write an explanation of the numeration system used by the Mayans. Complete the following tasks for this system:

1. Learn to read and write the symbols used by the Mayans. How would you write 5? 7? 20? 200? 360?

2. Enter the properties of the Mayan system on your chart.

3. Write a brief explanation of how the Mayan system works.

4. Examine all five systems studied in this unit and note which properties are present or absent for each one.

Guide: Use References 1, 2, 3, and 6 to obtain the necessary information. In addition, other encyclopedias and many books will contain sections or chapters on numeration systems.

Project 6

Our decimal system uses the code symbols 0, 1, 2, 3, 4, 5, 6, 7, 8, and 9, which are called *digits*. Each digit is exactly one, and only one, symbol. Write a brief explanation of the advantages of our decimal system over the ancient systems you have examined. Consider each of the following points:

1. The number of digits used
2. The writing of the numerals
3. The reading of the numerals
4. The circumstances under which regrouping becomes mandatory
5. The method of performing such operations as addition, subtraction, multiplication, and division
6. The use of zero in the decimal system

Guide: On the basis of the information you have collected, use logical reasoning skills and read Reference 4 (pp. 127–29) to aid you in writing your brief explanation. Explanations may vary as much as the individuals who consider the question. *Do not* underestimate your own original thinking.

Further Investigation

Develop a numeration system using only one symbol, such as the stroke (/) and the properties of addition, repetition, base, and place value. Consider the following points in order to complete the system:

1. Use as few strokes as possible to write the numerals.
2. Could the same numerals be written using more strokes than necessary?
3. What might you have to do to incorporate the property of place value?
4. Compare the advantages of our decimal system to the system you have developed.
5. Write numerals using more than one base.

Guide: Use the information that you have learned and also read Reference 5 (pp. 213–14).

REFERENCES

1. *Encyclopaedia Britannica*, s.v. "Numerals and Numeral Systems."
2. Freitag, Herta Taussig, and Arthur H. Freitag. *The Number Story*. Washington, D.C.: National Council of Teachers of Mathematics, 1960.
3. Johnson, Donovan A., and William H. Glenn. *Understanding Numeration Systems.* Saint Louis: Webster Division, McGraw-Hill Book Co., 1960.
4. Van Engen, Henry, Maurice L. Hartung, and James E. Stochl. *Foundations of Elementary School Arithmetic*. Chicago: Scott, Foresman & Co., 1965.
5. Van Engen, Henry, Maurice L. Hartung, Harold C. Trimble, Emil J. Berger, and Ray W. Cleveland. *Seeing through Mathematics, Book 1*. Glenview, Ill.: Scott, Foresman & Co., 1967.
6. Zoll, Edward J. *Systems of Numeration: A Programmed Text*. New York: Pitman Publishing Corp., 1968.

Teacher Notes

The purposes of the work with numeration systems are to (1) identify the properties associated with several ancient systems and (2) determine how the properties influence each of the systems. From this work, the student will be able to compare the ancient systems with our modern decimal system and understand that our system has certain advantages. For example, some of the ancient systems had the same properties as our present system but were somewhat more awkward to use. Another advantage of our modern system is the use of zero; the student will recognize how zero simplifies the expression of quantitative ideas.

To accomplish these purposes, the student is to complete a chart on the properties of each ancient system and understand how each property functions within the system. The student is to write a brief explanation of how each system works and give examples, if any, of how or where the system is used today.

The completed chart given below indicates the properties associated with each system. "X" notes the property is present.

Properties	Numeration Systems				
	Tally	Egyptian	Roman	Babylonian	Mayan
Addition	X	X	X	X	X
Repetition	X	X	X	X	X
Base		X	X	X	X
Place value				X	X

More detail as to how each property functions is provided in the discussion that follows. The students must understand and deal with each property that is present when writing their explanation. A possible sample student response for one system and notes for further investigations are provided.

Properties

The property of *addition* is used to determine the number being named. For example, the decimal numeral 231 tells us that we have 200 + 30 + 1. If we use a tally system when keeping score in a game, then / / / / becomes 1 + 1 + 1 + 1, or the quantity of 4.

The property of *repetition* provides that any symbol may be repeated as many times as needed when writing a given numeral. For example, in our decimal system the digit *1* is used three times to express the number 111. Again, simply put, any given symbol may be used as many times as needed.

If a system uses grouping to indicate quantities, then we have the property of a base. For example, in our decimal system grouping is done by tens. Ten ones can be regrouped as one ten and no ones: 10. The base is determined by the number by which you group, thus it is possible to group by twos, threes, fours, and so on, and to use any base you wish.

It is of interest to note that it is possible to group more than one way in some systems. When reading about the Roman system the student should note that the Romans grouped in more than one way.

When the value of a symbol is determined by its location within a group of symbols, the property of place value is in effect. For example, in the decimal numeral 111, the value of each digit is determined by where it is written. Beginning at the right, the first 1 is in the ones place, the second is in the tens place, and the third is in the hundreds place: 100 + 10 + 1 = 111. Thus the value of each 1 is different. The student should notice how much easier it is to write 111 in our system than in other systems.

One final point to be considered when studying the ancient systems is the use of subtraction in the Roman system. This is discussed in Reference 4.

Possible student response for tally system

A tally system uses a set of strokes to name a number of objects. When a numeral is written as a set of one or more strokes, then a tally numeral has been written. For example, to indicate 1, a single stroke is used. For the quantity 2, two strokes are used, and so forth. Writing the tally numerals from 1 to 10 would be as follows:

```
     /              //////
    //              ///////
   ///              ////////
  ////              /////////
 /////              //////////
```

Each stroke in a tally numeral expresses the number 1. Thus, the tally numeral expresses the sum of the ones, and so it has the property of *addition*. It also has the property of *repetition*, since the same symbol, the stroke, may be used more than once in a tally numeral.

Further Investigations

When using only one symbol to write numerals, the major problem that arises is the large number of strokes needed to express large quantities. How do you express large quantities without having to use a large number of strokes? This can be accomplished quite easily by utilizing the property of place value and some sort of device to indicate in what place the strokes are written. Consider the following:

$$/ \mid //// \mid /// \mid /$$

If the expression above is written using a base of ten, then the quantity expressed is our familiar decimal numeral 1431. Another way to look at the illustration is as follows:

/	////	///	/
$10 \times 10 \times 10$	10×10	10	1
10^3	10^2	10^1	10^0

Thus, the numeral in expanded form, using the familiar decimal digits, would be $1 (10^3) + 4 (10^2) + 3 (10^1) + 1 (10^0)$, or the neater 1431.

This same quantity could also be written as follows:

$$/ \mid //// \mid // \mid \begin{array}{c} ////// \\ ///// \end{array}$$

In expanded form this is $1 (10^3) + 4 (10^2) + 2 (10^1) + 11 (10^0)$, which becomes $1000 + 400 + 20 + 11$, or 1431. Therefore, it can be readily seen that in using such an approach, more strokes than are necessary can be written in a given place.